The entry of the Israelite tribes into Canaan, modest enough in its way, occurred in 1200-1180 B.C. The Bible account of these events is both literary and theological, but it deals with events which, beyond doubt, were historical.

We know that the Israelites had to fight hard to be able to settle in territory which was often far from what they expected of the Promised Land. But we can also be sure that, in addition to the fighting, there were also instances of cunning infiltration. Each tribe managed to make a place for itself on the map of Canaan, either side by side with, or on the fringes of the original population.

Yet two centuries after these events we find David, triumphantly seated on his throne as King of Israel, governing the Promised Land, formerly the land of Canaan, as absolute ruler. 1200 to 1000 B.C. — a mere two centuries. How can this

history and rich in lessons and revelations, are the subject of this volume.

Dr. Gaubert, assisted by a distinguished group of translators and Bible scholars representing the three major religious groups, is the author of the preceding Old Testament volumes in this series.

DAVID AND THE FOUNDATION OF JERUSALEM

This is VOLUME FOUR of

THE BIBLE IN HISTORY

A Contemporary Companion to the Bible

Edited by Father Robert Tamisier, P.S.S.

Advisory Editor for the English Language Edition: Joseph Rhymer

Editorial Consultants:

Father Edward J. Ciuba

Bishop John J. Dougherty

Rabbi Samuel Sandmel

Dr Samuel L. Terrien

David and the Foundation of Jerusalem

by HENRI GAUBERT

Translated by Lancelot Sheppard

A Giniger Book
published in association with
HASTINGS HOUSE, PUBLISHERS
NEW YORK

All inquiries should be addressed to Hastings House, Publishers, Inc., 10 East 40th Street, New York City 10016. This book was manufactured in Great Britain and published in association with The K. S. Giniger Company, Inc., New York City 10001. Library of Congress Catalog Card Number: 69-15814.
SBN: 8038-1537-9

CONTENTS

PREFACE

The Bible is a single book in which the pattern of God's work in his world can be traced through two thousand years of human history. There is a single pattern running through it all, and fundamentally it is a simple pattern. The complexity comes from the complexity of human history.

But the Bible is also a collection of books. Some of them grew out of folk tales, and stories from the nation's past, which were handed down from father to son, or told round the pilgrims' camp fires at the places where the people went to worship. Some of the books were written by men who can be named and placed in their historical situation, and some are anonymous and can only be given a firm date with difficulty. The whole collection grew slowly over many centuries, and was repeatedly edited and rearranged, until it reached the form in which we now have it.

This means that the Bible has never been a book which could be read without help. Even in New Testament times, people found parts of it obscure. Customs which are taken for granted, and ways of life which are accepted without question by people who have never known anything different, may be strange to the later reader and difficult to understand. This is more than ever true in our own times, when the society in which we live has changed so much, even during the last hundred years.

This present series of books is for use as a Companion to the Bible. They are not a substitute for the Bible, for nothing can take the place of the Bible itself. It impresses itself on those who read it seriously in a way that no other book can. Some of the difficulties about reading the Bible have been due to the way in which it has usually been printed. Many of these are overcome in the Jerusalem Bible, a translation in contemporary English which is used in this series. In the Jerusalem Bible the text is presented by dividing the books into sections, and providing headings and footnotes.

The aim of this present series of books is to help people to understand the divine revelation. It presents the Bible in the historical circumstances in which it developed. The men and women who were so acutely aware of God's active presence in their lives were all people of their times. Their experiences were the same as the experiences of their neighbours and fellow-countrymen. They earned their living by the same skills and trades, and their thoughts were expressed in the language used by everyone around them. To understand how God was revealing himself to these people, we must share their experiences as far as we can, and know what was happening in the world in which they lived.

Using the findings of archaeology and of historical research, the books in this series show the circumstances and the environment in which God made himself known. During recent years great advances have been made in our knowledge of the Near East during the period when the Bible was written, but these advances have only been possible because of the foundations laid patiently by scholars for more than a hundred years.

This series of books does not attempt to record all of the most recent finds, for new discoveries often have to be examined with caution before there can be certainty about their significance. Only those views which are accepted by a wide range of scholars are used here. It is impressive and reassuring to see how far the discoveries of the archaeologists and historians have confirmed the authenticity of details given in the Bible. Again and again, objects have been discovered, and sites have been excavated, which have confirmed the picture given by the Bible itself. There are many hindrances to archaeological work in the Near East. Political frontiers are often real barriers, and many important sites are still centres of worship where a thorough investigation is not possible. But we can be confident that new discoveries, as they are confirmed and analysed, will deepen our understanding of the times when the foundations of our religion were laid.

It is sometimes thought that books such as these should attempt to give the historical background to the Bible without any mention of God. This is impossible. The Bible is history, but it is also sacred history. It is history viewed and written with the knowledge that God is the active source of all history, and that all events are part of the movement towards the final consummation which God has willed. There is a pattern in the events of history, and God shows himself through this pattern. The events will not make sense, nor will they be worth studying, unless we see them from the point of view of the people who found God in them. We cannot make sense of the events if we leave God out.

The modern reader is sometimes surprised by the strange ways in which ancient historians presented their material, but much of this strangeness comes from the way in which ancient authors set about their task. Many of the writers of the Bible felt that their main responsibility was to preserve the traditions and the accounts of the events with as little alteration as possible. They were 'scribes' rather than authors. They copied out whatever information they could find, or selected the best descriptions and the parts that they thought mattered most. Then they stitched the pieces together without changing the words or the style.

They collected their information wherever they could find it, so their work contains poetry, epics, fiction, official chronicles, anecdotes, family and tribal memoirs, royal decrees, codes of law, letters, rules for priests. These, and many others, are the kind of sources which historians use in any age; they are the raw material of history, and without them the historian would be helpless. But in the ancient historian's writings this raw material has a marked effect on the way in which the history is written. There is much repetition and, sometimes, contradiction, when the 'author' uses two versions of the same event. But there is also a vivid immediacy about it all which helps us to come close to the people who took part in the event and to appreciate the effect it had upon them.

The account is presented to us in the people's own words, so we find that we can share more easily in their experiences, and appreciate more easily their point of view. It is the point of view of a people who recognised God's active presence, and who responded to his presence with worship.

Occasionally we can detect a further motive which has shaped some of the books of the Bible. The biblical writers were never mere historians. They only wrote about the past if it could throw light on their present situation. They wanted to show how God had acted in the past, so that the people of their own times could see God's presence and power at work in their own lives. So the biblical historians selected from the material available, and then arranged it so that the lessons were as obvious as it was possible to make them.

When we read these passages we are seeing the events of history through the eyes of men who frequently were writing about those events many generations after they had occurred. The books they wrote were expressions of the faith of the men who wrote them, and they were written to strengthen the faith of the people who read them. They have more to say about that faith than they have about the historical details of the events on which that faith was built.

Sometimes the books of the Bible contain deliberate anachronisms. This can be seen, for example, in some of the words and actions attributed to Moses. Moses had a greater influence on the Hebrew people than any other man. Later, in times of urgent need or of national reform, it was only natural for men to ask themselves what Moses would have done if he had been faced with their problems. The action taken, or the programme of reform, was then recorded as if Moses himself had foreseen the situation and had legislated for it. This is why so much of the law is written as if it had been given by Moses.

The men who wrote in this way were expressing an important truth. Whenever the nation was unfaithful to God, it was because it had forgotten the principles which Moses had taught to his generation of Hebrews. Those principles lay at the heart of the Hebrew faith, but the people of each new generation had to apply them to the changing circumstances of their times. The convention of making Moses the author of all their laws was the clearest way of showing that those laws were expressions of the central traditions of the nation.

The people of the Bible recognised the thread of God's revelation in the ordinary events of their lives. This series of books shows what those events were, and how that thread fits into its historical background. Each book may be read on its own, but the books are also linked together to form a continuous exposition and elucidation of the way in which God has made himself known through the Bible. The titles in the series are:

Volume 1: ABRAHAM, LOVED BY GOD
Volume 2: ISAAC AND JACOB, GOD'S CHOSEN ONES
Volume 3: MOSES AND JOSHUA, FOUNDERS OF THE NATION
Volume 4: DAVID AND THE FOUNDATION OF JERUSALEM
Volume 5: SOLOMON THE MAGNIFICENT
Volume 6: THE DESTRUCTION OF THE KINGDOM
Volume 7: THE REBIRTH OF ISRAEL
Volume 8: JESUS THE GALILEAN
Volume 9: JESUS AND HIS DISCIPLES
Volume 10: THE PASCHAL COMMUNITY
Volume 11: THE CHURCH OF PENTECOST
Volume 12: ST PAUL AND THE CHURCH

Each book contains the necessary maps, diagrams and illustrations for the period with which it is concerned. The reader is also recommended to use the chronological table, the maps and the general information printed after the New Testament in the Jerusalem Bible Standard Edition.

Joseph Rhymer,
Editor of the English Language Edition.

INTRODUCTION

In about 1200 B.C. the tribes of Israel – Moses' nomad shepherds who for 'forty years' (a symbolic number) had been wandering on the Sinai Peninsula – crossed over the Jordan opposite Jericho. Then these still primitive tribes attacked the Canaanite civilization with eager confidence.

Precarious establishment of the Israelites in the Promised Land

The Land of Canaan was the Promised Land, promised by Yahweh to Abraham for his remote descendants and as a reward for his faith. It was a family property, in some sort, over which Israel possessed, and there was no doubt about it among the Israelites, undeniable rights.

To Joshua and his men at arms who had recently won resounding victories over the pastoral peoples of Transjordania, the campaign which they were beginning to the west of the Jordan and the Dead Sea would be swift and decisive. But they soon had to tell another tale.

Israel loses on all sides

The situation was very unfavourable for the Israelite invader. During the past centuries Egypt had exercised overlordship over Canaan. To ensure the proper administration of the country the Egyptian government

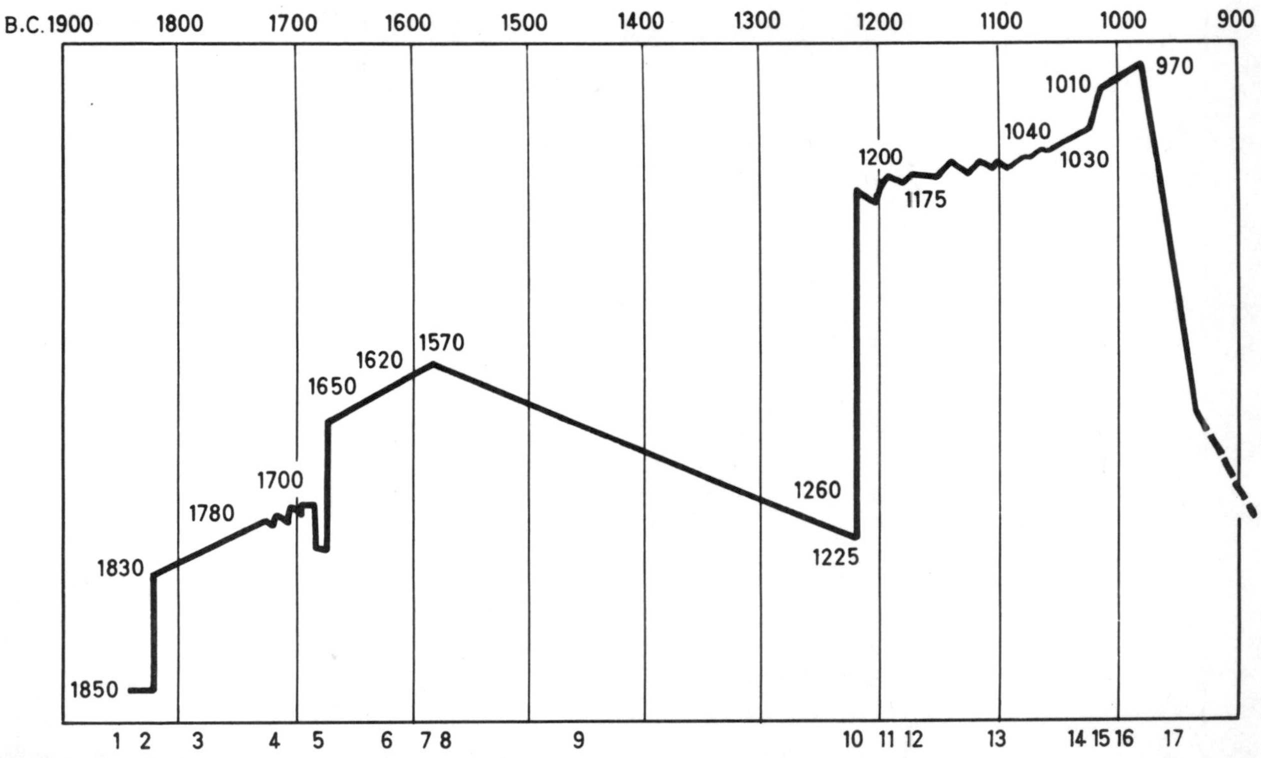

B.C. 1900
1800
1700
1600
1500
1400
1300
1200
1100
1000
900
970
1010
1040
1030
1200
1175
1570
1620
1650
1700
1780
1830
1850
1260
1225
1 2 3 4 5 6 7 8 9 10 11 12 13 14 15 16 17

GRAPH OF THE SPIRITUAL ASCENT OF THE PEOPLE OF ISRAEL

The only purpose of this outline is to give a general idea of the spiritual development of the people of Israel. After Joshua (1200–1175) the graph sums up the historical sequence which will be dealt with in later works in this series of volumes.

We are concerned here with the spiritual ascent alone; it does not always coincide, far from it, with material advance. Thus, during the four hundred years spent in the Wadi Tumilat (9) the conditions of life obviously improved, but the idea of a mission grew weak. On the other hand, during the 'forty years' spent in the desert (10–11) with Moses, an opposite effect can be observed; the harsh material existence led gradually to a revival of the sense of vocation among the Hebrews.

It should be noted that in ancient history before 600 B.C. dates cannot be determined with any accuracy. They are given here merely as an indication.

ABRAHAM: (1850–1780?), son of Terah.

1. About 1850, Abraham leaves Ur, in company with the clan of his father Terah.
2. About 1830, at Haran, the revelation to Abraham of the one, holy, invisible God.

ISAAC: (*c.* 1780–1700?), son of Abraham.

3. His life is not marked by any striking event.

JACOB: (*c.* 1700?–1620?), son of Isaac.

4. The troubles that marked the patriarch's early days.
5. The crossing of the Jabbok.
6. Jacob understands his mission.

JOSEPH: (1700?–1620?), son of Jacob.

7. Joseph arrives in the Egyptian Delta, occupied at that period by the Hyksos and their Asiatic collaborators.
8. Jacob and his sons come down to the Delta.
9. For about four centuries the Israelites remain in the Delta area.

MOSES:

10. About 1225, the Exodus or departure from Egypt in the reign of the pharaoh Meneptah. The crossing of the Red Sea. Sojourn for about a year near Sinai.
Kadesh.
Death of Moses on Mount Nebo (*c.* 1200).

JOSHUA:

11. About 1200 the Hebrews cross the Jordan in the neighbourhood of Jericho.
12. From 1200 to 1175, the tribes of Israel settle in Canaan.

PERIOD OF THE JUDGES:

13. 1175–1040, the Judges.
14. 1040–1030, Samuel.

THE KINGSHIP:

15. 1030–1010, Saul.
16. 1010–970, David.
17. 970–931, Solomon.

made use of native Semite chieftains who were employed as high officials. Now at the time of Moses and Joshua the Egyptians had begun to experience difficult times and with all the manpower at their disposal had to repulse the attacks on the Delta by the People of the Sea. At once the former Canaanite governors took advantage of the weakening of Egyptian power to transform themselves into petty independent feudal lords. They were established in strong fortresses surrounded by enormous walls (some of them were twenty-five, twenty-six or even thirty feet thick), flanked with towers placed at strategic points; then in addition there were the glacis, the outworks, and deep trenches – medieval military architects in the West could hardly have done better. How were the Israelites with the inadequate arms and equipment of shepherds to overcome these formidable strongholds? The Bible certainly mentions a few victorious actions by the Israelites against these fortresses, but these were quite exceptional, and their success could be explained as the result of surprise or treachery.

The Canaanite cities, too, were strongly fortified. On the approach of the enemy the countryfolk from the neighbourhood would hurriedly seek refuge in the city, taking with them stocks of corn and their flocks.

In the plains also Israel would find themselves fighting at a disadvantage; like Egypt and Mesopotamia, the Canaanite chiefs possessed powerful formations of chariots. These two-wheeled vehicles were drawn by spirited horses; in addition to the driver they carried one or two skilled archers. The chariots were almost like light tanks; they mowed down the lines of infantry. Tactically the Israelites were on the losing side.

On account of their undeniable military inferiority the theoretical owners of the Promised Land had to be content with those parts of the country which were of absolutely no interest to the masters of the country: the mountain regions occupied by the remnants of the pre-Canaanite populations, certain wooded districts which had not yet been cleared, or else the semi-wildernesses which were wanted by no one.

In short, the Canaanites remained undisputed masters of the country.

The Israelite tribes, obliged to settle where they could, were separated from each other; sometimes they were even isolated from their Yahwistic co-religionists. On the other hand, social contacts with the Canaanites continually increased. From these latter in fact the Israelites were to learn the rudiments of agriculture (planting of fruit trees, care of the vine), of architecture (building of houses and subsequently of fortifications), and of craftsmanship (textiles, pottery). Between the newcomers and the inhabitants of the country friendly relations were soon established – both were Semites and fairly closely related – and also commercial relations; very soon, too, there were cases of inter-marriage. The assimilation of the former Israelite nomads was, it appeared, only a question of a few generations. On the social level Israel was certainly losing.

At the religious level the situation was still more disquieting. For among the Semites the farmer worshipped the deity who protected his field, the city-dweller the deity protecting his city. If a man changed from farmer to citizen or vice versa he had to invoke the god established in the region of his new residence. The Israelites did not forget their God Yahweh, but the Semitic customs influenced them when they entered the Promised Land and made acquaintance with the polytheistic pantheon to be found there. What gods did they find in fact in Canaan?

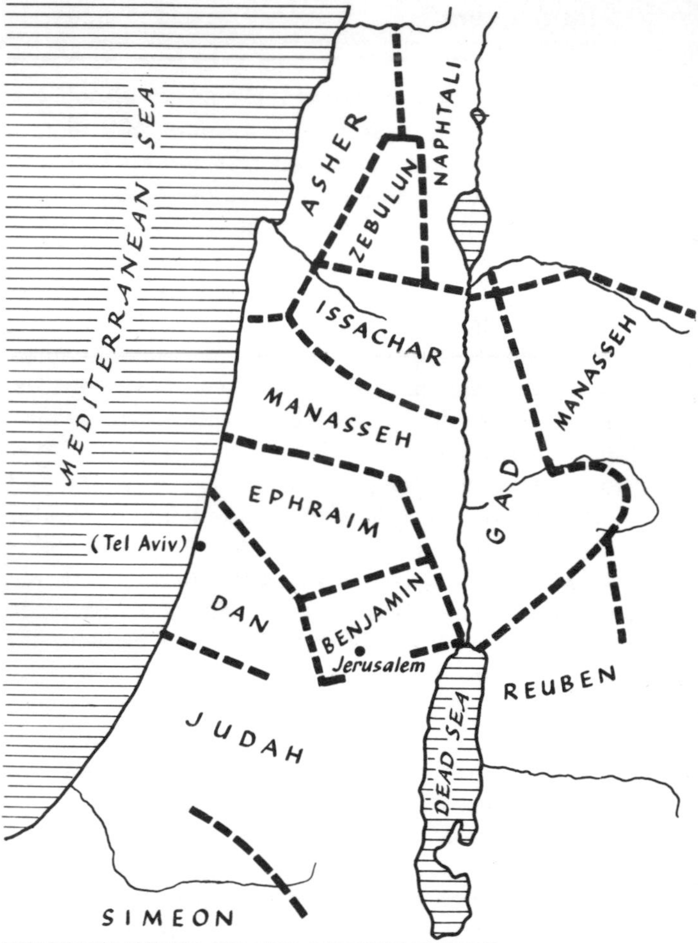

ESTABLISHMENT OF THE TWELVE TRIBES AT THE TIMES OF THE JUDGES (1200–1030 B.C.)

This is the traditional plan and is intended to give a general idea of the settlement of the tribes of Israel in Canaan at the time of the Judges. There can be no question in the circumstances of talking about total conquest. The invading Israelite tribes only occupied certain mountainous regions, or very poor districts – that is, the regions that the Canaanites left to them. In fact, the groups of Israelites were very often at a distance from each other, and sometimes even isolated. The sketch map above must only be seen as merely a rough indication of the zones of influence in which each tribe, during the coming centuries, was to work for the constitution of a unified kingdom.

In the first place 'El, also called Baal-Shamin, the god of heaven. This powerful personage had three sons: Sharar (Morning Star), Shalem (Evening Star), Sedek (Justice of god). Among the local gods was Dagon, the god of corn; although of Mesopotamian origin, he was adopted by the Philistines. There was also the famous Moloch; he was a tireless destroyer who thought only of peopling his kingdom which was that of the dead; for this purpose he started wars, and provoked famines and plague. But he could be appeased to some extent by the offering of human sacrifices. And then there was the famous Astarte, the goddess of fertility.

In fact each locality possessed its Baal, the master, the owner of the soil, a sort of feudal lord to whom a portion of the produce of the land had to be paid. Hence the sacrifices offered to him by the farmer with the first ears of corn harvested and the first-born of the flock; hence, too, the offering to him by the head of the family of his first-born son. Baal was supposed to be particularly exacting about what were known as 'foundation' sacrifices; when a house was built, to obtain the good graces of the deity a small child had to be placed alive in a jar of ashes and buried in a cavity in the foundations of the building. Archaeologists have discovered these small skeletons in the underground walls of dwellings.

All these rites struck the imagination of the Israelites very forcibly. Although the articles of the Decalogue, clearly explained at length by the Mosaic Law, forbade all practices of this kind, only too often it was not long before Israelites adopted them. They felt that they had to placate the gods to whom the territory belonged.

Sometimes they allowed themselves to be led astray by their Canaanite friends and attended ceremonies organized on the high places or near springs beneath the shade of the sacred trees. There, on a stele (the raised stone always provoked a religious feeling among the Semites) oil was ritually poured. Elsewhere, on an altar before a statue, sacrifices were offered. The celebration usually concluded in the company of the sacred prostitutes.

The Israelites did not, it is true, forget Yahweh; he always remained the God of Israel. But his worship, carefully codified by Moses, was very austere. He was an invisible God and the exacting moral requirements of the Decalogue were truly difficult to observe. Thus, while at the bottom of their hearts the Israelites preserved the revelation of the patriarchs, they allowed themselves gradually to be seduced by the orgiastic and idolatrous practices of the Canaanites.

Logically, Yahwism should have disappeared fairly rapidly beneath the materialistic wave of the attractive and powerful old Semitic religion. Militarily, socially and religiously Israel was losing. The future seemed dark.

King David of Judah and Israel, reigning in Jerusalem

By the year 1000, two centuries after the events described, the political, social and religious situation of the Israelites was to be seen in an entirely new and unexpected light. By then the land of Canaan was wholly under the absolute dominion of the former Israelite invaders and it was they who enacted the law. David, king of Judah and Israel, appeared as an absolute sovereign, governing with authority a unified nation which was fulfilling its religious vocation in the Promised Land. In his capital Jerusalem David inaugurated the tenth century with the brilliant victory of Yahwism over the temporal power of the Canaanites. The champions of the ancient Semitic idolatry had at last been defeated.

Two centuries sufficed to obtain this extraordinary and unbelievable change. Two centuries: from Joshua (1200) to David (1000), were sufficient for this victorious progress, though it did not exclude difficulties, reverses, tragedies and even comedies. These two centuries form the object of this study.

The four stages of Israel's progress towards unity and kingship (1200–1000)

This period of history during which Israel succeeded in establishing its political unity is considered in the four following chapters. Each of these stages possessed its own clear characteristics.

The first stage is the period of the Judges. It lasted for nearly one and a half centuries (1175–1040) and was made up of sporadic, scattered efforts which were sometimes blundering but often heroic. Israel began to realise that it had to attain a political unity if it would save from oblivion the spiritual message entrusted to it.

The second stage was that of Samuel the prophet (about 1040–1030). During it Israel began to experience the need for a political and religious head, for, in fact, a king. But there was still some hesitation – after all, was not Yahweh the sovereign and guide of the Twelve Tribes?

The third stage was that of Saul (1030–1010); it represented the first attempt at royal power. Despite the undeniable worth of this sovereign the venture was cut short.

The fourth stage brings us to David (1010–970). He was outstanding as a political and military genius, an exceptional diplomat, a great religious leader and an able administrator. In addition, he was helped considerably by circumstances. Under the impulsion of this dynamic and powerful personality – David must be regarded as one of the most accomplished sovereigns of all times – Israel attained the summit of its power.

Judges, Samuel, Saul and David: four chapters in which we can witness the great rise of Yahwism as a social and religious force.

1

THE PERIOD OF THE JUDGES (1175–1040 B.C.)

In the Bible after the Book of Joshua comes the Book of Judges. It is an account, in anecdotal form, of the Israelite 'resistance' to the Canaanite ascendancy. The very existence of the People of God was at stake. The situation was extremely serious.

Israel's inner strength

The religious traditions of these former nomads now began to take shape in epic accounts, the improvised compositions of the survivors of the adventure on Sinai. Moses' shepherds, in stories which very rapidly assumed a fixed, stereotyped form, told their grandchildren the amazing history of the People of God, protected by Yahweh and led across the plains by Moses, Yahweh's prophet. But all that was of the past. Life had changed from what it had been during the exciting period in the wilderness when the religious ideal took shape, matured and grew daily clearer through the direct, incessant action of Moses, the man who talked with Yahweh 'face to face'. Yet it should not be concluded too rapidly that shortly after Joshua's time Yahwism was on the wane. The memory of the Covenant concluded between Yahweh and his people remained vivid, at least in some quarters.

It did so, in the first place, among the priests of Shiloh, a high place situated to the south of Shechem. There, in safety, lay the Ark of the Covenant, the protection of the Twelve Tribes. A body of priests was in charge of this sacred chest in which were kept the stone tablets of the Law.

Among devout families, too, the traditions of Yahwism were carefully preserved. And also among the Levites who had become the custodians of the places of pilgrimage. They were to be found scattered about in various centres where their office was liturgical in nature. Although their orthodoxy was not always free from criticism they remained nevertheless servants of the altar and the archivists of the Law of Moses and of the great religious events of their people.

There were also the 'Sons of the Prophets' or *nabis*.[1] They were a kind of religious confraternity whose members were bound by temporary or permanent vows according to individual cases. They wore their hair long, abstained from all fermented liquor and regarded themselves as consecrated to the service of Yahweh. They formed centres of faith in which Yahweh was venerated as the only saviour of his people.

To conclude this list of the little islands of Israelite resistance the 'Judges' must also be mentioned, those national heroes and envoys whose personal action was to transform the whole period of history to which very rightly their name has been given.

The Judges: definition of the term

The Judges: *shophetim;* in the singular, *shophet*. The term can be compared with Suffete which, at Tyre and Carthage (centres of Canaanite-Phoenician origin)

[1] There should also be mentioned the *nazirs* who were consecrated to Yahweh.

designated the political heads of the city who were elected for a term. But the biblical 'Judge' must not be thought of as a magistrate responsible for passing sentence or giving judgement, for that office among most of the settled Semites devolved on the council of elders, who usually sat in the public square near the principal gate of the city.

The 'Judge' in the Bible was *he who makes the law* (of Yahweh) *triumph*. He was a 'judge-saviour' chosen by God to effect a 'deliverance'. In France Joan of Arc, for example, is comparable to these 'inspired' men of the Old Testament; they were simple folk who, usually, received their mission very unexpectedly; men who, 'being seized by the spirit of God', communicated their enthusiasm to their own circle, galvanizing their fellows into action, encouraged the hesitant to fight and led their people to victory.

The Judge was therefore a military leader with authority for only a limited period; during the time when he was in power he was responsible for imposing by force the rights of the People of God on the Land of Canaan, the Promised Land.

The Judges: the historical picture of the period

To an historian, who must endeavour to see beyond the anecdotal character of the Book of Judges, it appears as a slow, clumsy, almost chaotic progress leading eventually to the establishment of kingship.

At first we find a few Israelite groups of the north and centre of Palestine who became allies in order to ward off a common danger. A military leader was therefore chosen to lead into battle the troops of a few of the Israelite tribes. But directly after the campaign the leader in question had to return to the ranks, or, more properly speaking, to take up again his agricultural pursuits with his fields and cattle. In these conditions Israel could not achieve much else besides very mediocre and temporary successes.

Yet after several bitter experiences Israel finally began to understand how necessary it was to have a single military command at the head of the Twelve Tribes. The complete, definitive victory of the sons of Jacob could only be achieved at this price, and the better minds among them were beginning to realize this.

The Judges: the theological context

During the long and arduous period of the settlement in Canaan (twelfth century and a good part of the eleventh) the Chosen People might well expect, almost it would seem by definition, to be greatly helped by Yahweh, its God and its Protector. On the contrary, we find Israel plunged into great difficulties, a fact which caused some astonishment to the faithful among the Israelites. The Deuteronomist theologians of the seventh century undertook the task of furnishing the necessary explanations.

If, from time to time, they tell us in substance, the Hebrew tribes were cut in pieces, vanquished or made vassals by the enemy it was only justice; Israel had strayed from the Mosaic Law and suffered the just punishment for its sins. Yahweh abandoned his people to their merely human strength and they immediately failed. But let Israel once repent of the evil that it had done, let it 'call on Yahweh' and he would forgive and raise up a 'judge', a military leader who was Yahweh's envoy, whose responsibility it would be to rally the people and save them from the danger which threatened them.

Of course, some years after each recovery Israel fell once more into the same sins and the process began again. That is the theme of the Book of Judges. This theological explanation was set out by Fr Lagrange in the form of a sequence with four stages: Sin – Punishment – Repentance – Forgiveness.

1. Sin. Israel transgressed the Law of Moses (by worship of the Baals, taking part in the orgiastic cults of the idolators, marriage with the Canaanites).

2. Punishment. Yahweh turns away from his people; Israel's enemies at once take advantage of the withdrawal of divine protection to reduce one or other of the Israelite tribes to slavery.[2]

3. Repentance. Under the blows of misfortune falling so heavily upon them the Israelites, realizing their transgressions, 'call on Yahweh' and implore his mercy.

4. Forgiveness. Yahweh, touched by these sincere marks of repentance sends, for this or that group of tribes which are especially threatened, a judge who will lead them to victory.

That is the pattern of each judgeship. Yet this theological plan, despite its utility for the reader of the Bible, does not help us much at the historical level which we must now examine.

The Twelve Judges

The number twelve was decided upon to give satisfaction to each of the Twelve Tribes of Israel. Sometimes indeed the scribe was in obvious difficulties in placing certain vague personages; in that case he took refuge in a brief summary; at other times he was in possession of full sources of information and could give reign to his

[2] At this period, it should be remembered, the Israelites still retained the primitive, not to say naive, idea of *earthly* retribution for Good or Evil. The righteous man was rewarded here below; the wicked man was punished during his life. God's justice was manifested at a purely human and strictly earthly level. It was only in the third century B.C. and especially in the second century, that belief grew in rewards and punishments *after* death.

literary abilities. Among the twelve Judges mentioned in the Bible there were only four great national heroes: Deborah, Gideon, Jephthah and Samson. These enable us to penetrate a little into the historical situation and the lives of the Israelites during this period known as the 'Conquest'.

Deborah: the greatest leader in the Book of Judges (about 1125)

After the vigorous but very brief interventions of the three first Judges – Othniel (3: 7–11), Ehud (3: 12–30), and Shamgar (3: 31) – there appears the brilliant personality of Deborah ('the bee'), prophetess and liberator. We can here follow Fr Lagrange and see the four stages of development within the context of Deborah's judgeship.

First stage: the Sin. *Once again the Israelites* [this is the term used in the Bible but it was, as a matter of fact, the tribe of Ephraim] *began to do what displeases Yahweh* (Judg. 4: 1). Once again it was a case of the worship of Canaanite idols or compromising with the rulers of the country.

Second stage: Punishment. *Yahweh handed them over* [that is, after being vanquished in battle] *to Jabin* one of the kings of Canaan *who reigned at Hazor* (south-west of Lake Huleh). For twenty years Ephraim was reduced to a state of vassalage by this ruler.

Third stage: Repentance. *Then the Israelites cried to Yahweh*. In other words, they acknowledged their serious infractions of the Law and expressed their repentance before Yahweh.

Fourth stage: Forgiveness. Yahweh raised up a Judge – in this case, Deborah – who delivered the unfortunate Israelites from their vassal state.

'You are a large population and one of great strength . . . a mountain shall be yours; it is covered with woods, but you must clear it, and its boundaries shall be yours, since you cannot drive out the Canaanite because of his iron chariots and his superior strength.'

Joshua 17:18

At this time Deborah . . ., a prophetess, . . . used to sit under Deborah's Palm between Ramah and Bethel in the highlands of Ephraim, and the Israelites would come to her to have their disputes decided (Judg. 4: 4–5).

Two preliminary remarks are necessary here. In the first place, it should be pointed out that this office of 'judge' (chieftain) assumed by Deborah had nothing in common with the lofty mission of 'Judge in Israel' with which she was subsequently invested. Then, it seems a little surprising to find a woman occupying such an important position; usually in the East women were relegated to material tasks. But there can be no doubt about the truth of the matter here.

With this in mind we can examine the situation more closely. It appears that the real issue at stake was the Plain of Jezreel (or Esdraelon, sometimes called the Plain of Megiddo), a large area of red and black clay. On it were situated the fine farms belonging to the Canaanite landed proprietors. A line of forts defended this cultivated land against possible incursions of nomads from the east, known as the 'Sons of the East', who were invariably attracted by the harvest and raided the region. In the strong points, securely perched on the hills, the 'feudal' overlords kept watch and, in return for a tax on the harvests, guaranteed the peasants peace and tranquility in the region.

The Israelite tribes of the north and centre, pushed back into the mountains, may well have looked enviously on these rich farms on which fine crops of wheat, barley, oats and millet were grown. Some clans managed to settle quietly in the plain (Judg. 1: 27–34), and established themselves on a modest scale, though they did not dare a frontal attack on the chariots and troops guarding the country. Eventually this peaceful infiltration was bound to attract the attention of the Canaanite proprietors. A collision was inevitable before long.

Deborah, the Bible tells us, then received from Yahweh the order to proclaim war. Only six tribes answered the call of this new Judge: Ephraim, Benjamin and Manasseh, Zebulun, Issachar and Naphtali. Reuben and Gad, settled in Transjordania, preferred to remain with their flocks; Dan and Asher, probably reduced to slavery by the Phoenicians of Tyre and Sidon were obliged to stay where they were. The defection, or rather the absence, of Judah and Simeon can be understood; these two tribes were settled far away to the south in the Negeb and were not in regular touch with their kinsmen. Thus only a half of Israel took part in the campaign launched by Deborah. To lead the Israelite troops into battle she chose one Barak, (lightning), a native of Kedesh in Naphtali. In Yahweh's name she ordered him to attack. He accepted the position on condition that Deborah accompanied him to the battlefield, probably because he felt that he might need the inspirations of the prophetess during the fighting.

The action took place at the foot of Mount Tabor on the Plain of Jezreel to the south of Mount Carmel near the Kishon, a small fast-flowing coastal river.[3] Sisera, the leader of the Canaanite troops, brought out his chariots which terrified the Israelite infantry. But Deborah encouraged her men and imbued them with such enthusiasm as to ensure victory. Barak was camping with his troops on Mount Tabor. *'Up!'* she commanded him, *'For today is the day Yahweh has put*

[3] This plain, about twenty-four miles wide and sixteen long, was the normal battlefield of Palestine. On several occasions the Egyptian and Assyrian armies confronted each other there, as did the Israelites and Canaanites; in the Middle Ages the Crusaders fought there against the Saracens. Bonaparte's decisive victory over the Turks occurred at Mount Tabor (1799).

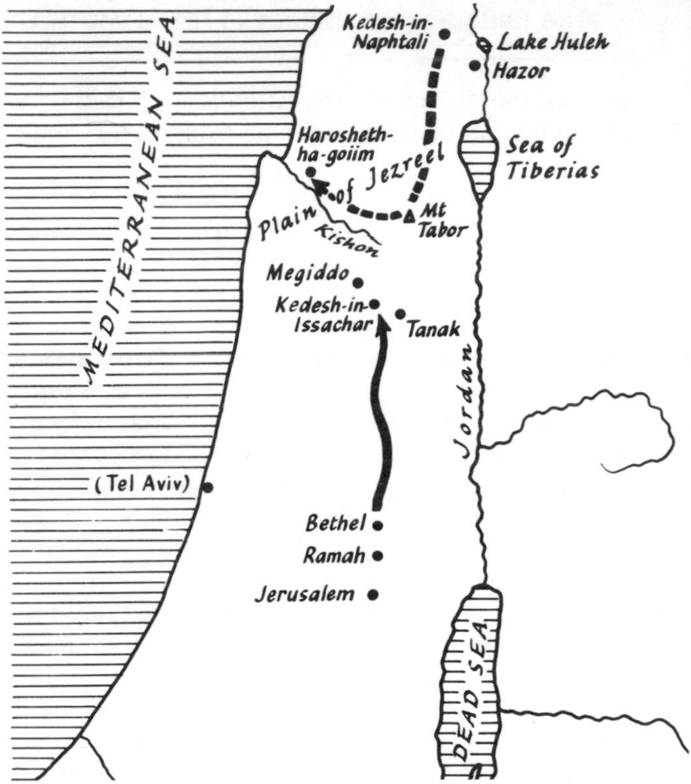

JUDGESHIP OF DEBORAH.
THE VICTORIOUS CAMPAIGN OF CERTAIN TRIBES OF ISRAEL AT THE KISHON (about 1125)

Certain Canaanite leaders planned a campaign against the Israelite tribes who were beginning to settle in the fertile plain of Jezreel. Deborah, who gave her oracles beneath an oak tree between Ramah and Bethel, called the Twelve Tribes to arms. Only six of them answered the summons. Israel's army was under the orders of Barak, a native of Kedesh in Naphtali. The Canaanites were commanded by Sisera (he lived at Harosheth-ha-goiim), head of the army of Jabin, king of Hazor.

Barak drew up his plan of battle in agreement with Deborah at Kedesh in Issachar. Barak came down from the north with the Israelite troops that he managed to gather together and lay in wait on Mount Tabor. The battle took place on both sides of the Kishon: at Tanak, Megiddo, across the Kishon and as far as Harosheth-ha-goiim.

Sisera into your power. Yes, Yahweh marches at your head.' The Israelites rushed down the hillside; panic-stricken, the enemy fled; part of the Canaanites *fell by the edge of the sword*; another part drowned in trying to cross the Kishon, at that time swollen as the result of a terrible but providential storm.[4]

Sisera leapt from his chariot and fled on foot.

Worn out, he came to a camp of Kenites (the picturesque metalworkers of the desert whom we have already encountered at the time of Moses). They were Semites, kinsmen of the Israelites, but not at that time at war with the Canaanites. There were no men in the camp as they were all at work, guarding the flocks on the plain nearby. The fugitive appealed to Jael, wife of Heber, chieftain of the clan, and asked her for a drink of water; she gave him a bowl of *leben*, a kind of sour milk and, as if to hide him from the searchers, she covered him with a rug. '*Do not be afraid*,' she said. Then, when she thought that Sisera was asleep, she took a tent-peg and a mallet, crept up to the Canaanite leader and drove the peg through his temple. *And so he died*. Shortly afterwards Barak arrived in pursuit of his rival. '*Come in*,' Jael said to him, '*and I will show you the man you are looking for*.' It was a particularly despicable murder, directly contrary to the sacred laws of hospitality. And yet the Bible has not one word of blame for Jael, indeed she is called 'blessed among women'. The scribe who wrote this account probably regarded her as an instrument of the justice of God.

Such was the first attempt at unity on the part of the

[4] The Kishon is formed by the junction of several streams which wind their way across the valley. Its mouth is in the bay of Haifa. The Kishon is not more than about thirty feet wide, but it flows between two steep cliffs, at places as much as twelve to sixteen feet high. In the immediate neighbourhood of Mount Tabor, where the battle took place, the various streams transform this part of the plain into marshland at the time of the floods.

Israelite tribes. It had a twofold result. In the first place there was the political victory which gained the Israelites relative independence from the Canaanites in the northern part of the country. Then there was the moral victory by which thenceforward the house of Jacob could feel sure that Yahweh would enable it to meet even the most formidable ordeals. Nationalism and faith were combined in a single ideal. This was the first taste of victories in the not too distant future.

This memorable battle for the capture of the Plain of Jezreel is described by the Book of Judges in two versions, one in prose and the other poetical. The prose account is regarded by modern biblical scholars as the work of a Yahwistic scribe of the southern part of the country; they consider it to have been composed at a later period (seventh century). The poetic version, on the other hand, goes back to ancient times; it might even be contemporary with the events described. In any case, by general agreement it is regarded as being one of the most beautiful literary masterpieces of the Old Testament. Certain statements and several allusions tend to show that it is the work of a woman and poetess who experienced the events described at first hand, and there is good reason to think that the author of the celebrated 'Song' was, in fact, Deborah herself.

Whatever the truth of the matter this magnificent poem brings out clearly the cosmic dimension that some of the more advanced Israelites were beginning to attribute to Yahweh; he was no longer merely a tribal God (the idea very generally held hitherto by Abraham's descendants) but a universal God, master of heaven and earth. And in response to this loving protection with which the 'God of Sinai' was pleased to surround his chosen people – so long, at least, as they kept the

Law – there can be observed on the human side, that is, in the Song of Deborah, a very moving feeling of genuine love; it was still rudimentary perhaps, but it marked a definite stage in the spiritual history of humanity.

Gideon, Judge in Israel (about 1120; approximately the same period as Deborah). See map, p. 14.

The days of hardship and trial returned; the Bible tells us why and how: once again we find the theological development in four stages.

Sin. *The Israelites did what displeases Yahweh.*

Punishment. For seven years *Yahweh gave over* [the tribes of the north] *into the hands of Midian*, the nomads from Transjordania, the 'Sons of the East'; mounted on their fast-moving camels they carried out swift and successful raids from this side of the Jordan; they destroyed *the produce of the country as far as Gaza; they left Israel nothing to live on, not a sheep or ox or donkey.*

Repentance. *The Israelites cried to Yahweh.*

Forgiveness of the sinner. Yahweh, after addressing bitter reproaches to his people (*'Do not reverence the gods of the Amorites'. 'You have not listened to my words', 'I am Yahweh your God'*) sends Gideon to give protection to the Israelite clans so hardly treated by the robbers on the plains.

Gideon was a poor peasant of the village of Ophrah to the south-west of the Lake of Gennesaret, near Mount Tabor. On the day in question he had secretly begun to thresh wheat which was scarcely ripe; he was concerned to get the grain to a place of safety before the arrival of Midianite brigands whose raid was to be expected at that season of the year. Suddenly, a few paces away, Gideon observed the *angel of Yahweh*

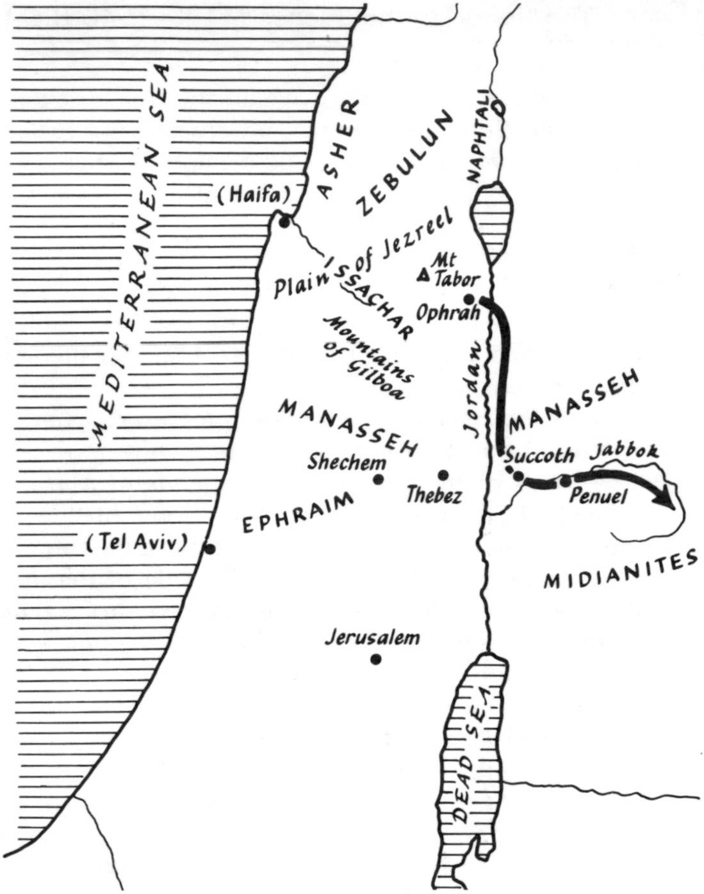

CAMPAIGN OF GIDEON THE 'JUDGE' AGAINST THE MIDIANITES (about 1120)

At Ophrah (south-west of the Lake of Gennesaret in the Mount Tabor region) Gideon, a young peasant, was threshing his corn when unexpectedly he received from Yahweh the task of repulsing the Midianite raiders who each year brought desolation to the plain of Jezreel. With a handful of followers Gideon crossed over to the left bank of the Jordan and followed down the course of the river. At Succoth (a little to the north of the Jabbok) and at Penuel (on the bank of the river) Gideon's co-religionists refused to supply his troops with food. Gideon defeated the Midianites at the mouth of the Jabbok. On the return journey he exacted terrible vengeance from the inhabitants of Penuel and Succoth.

seated beneath a terebinth tree. *'Yahweh is with you,'* said the mysterious visitor by way of greeting, but received a sharp reply. *'If Yahweh is with us . . . where are all the wonders our ancestors tell us of . . . Egypt? . . . Sinai? . . . Now Yahweh has deserted us. He has abandoned us to Midian.'* A serious argument followed. More than once Gideon asked his visitor to furnish tangible proof of his supernatural origin. Patiently, and contrary to his usual manner of dealing with similar cases, Yahweh complied with the requests of Gideon. The Book of Judges paints the scene vividly.

It was time to act. The Midianites on their camels had just invaded the Plain of Jezreel. Gideon decided to 'sound the horn' (a hollowed out goat's horn producing a harsh note which could be heard over a long distance and was used to give the signal for the beginning of a battle). By the dispatch of messengers the new Judge succeeded in gathering round him, in addition to his own tribe of Issachar, the neighbouring tribe of Manesseh as well as the warriors of Asher, Zebulun and Naphtali (see map, page 14).

Soon in fact he had too many soldiers. After a careful choice (its method was not without its picturesque side) he sent back to their fields and their vines all those he considered unsuitable for his secret expedition.

Gideon retained merely three hundred soldiers. At the appointed time each of these men was provided with an empty pitcher in which had been hidden a lighted torch. They were divided up into three groups of a hundred each and advanced noiselessly at dead of night towards the Midianite camp, approaching it from three different points. Just at the moment when the guard was being changed at the camp, Gideon sounded his horn. At once his men broke their pitchers and seized their torches in their left hands; with their right they raised their horns and blew a mightly blast. Terrified by the din and the unexpected lights the Midianites rushed from their tents and in their fright began fighting each other; finally they fled in disorder. Gideon hastened to warn the tribe of Ephraim to defend the water-points and in following this advice they succeeded in capturing the two Midianite chieftains Oreb (raven) and Zeeb (wolf). And they had every hope very shortly of wiping out the remainder of the Midianites.

Here we can observe how tenuous was the bond of brotherhood between the various Israelite groups. We have just seen the Ephraimites come on the scene in response to Gideon's summons. They had not forgotten that their eponymous ancestor, Ephraim, was the *younger* son of Joseph the Egyptian, specially singled out and blessed by his grandfather Jacob before his elder brother Manasseh. And so the Ephraimites were often contemptuous of the other members of the family, they did not hide their aspirations to leadership or even their tendency to separatism. Thus they adopted a haughty tone with the peasant leader of the tiny tribe of Issachar who, on his own account, had decided to wage a holy war against the common enemy, the nomad Midianites. Gideon was clever enough to extricate himself from this difficult situation: '*Into your power Yahweh has given the chieftains of Midian, Oreb and Zeeb,*' he told them. '*Can what I managed to do compare with what you have done?*' His words calmed their anger. It is clear that Israel was far from that national unity which was then very necessary for them.

There was another typical example of this lack of solidarity. During a second campaign against the Midianites, but this time on the other bank of the

Jordan,[5] Gideon's men, who obviously had no supply lines, were hungry, thirsty and exhausted. Gideon asked the citizens of Succoth (of the Israelite tribe of Gad) for *a few loaves of bread*. He explained that he was pursuing Zebah and Zalmunna, the kings of Midian. The elders of Succoth answered ironically: *'Are the hands of Zebah and Zalmunna already in your grasp?'* (The hands of a vanquished enemy, it should be explained, were cut off.) And the citizens, on the fortifications, invited Gideon and his men to go on their way. To this insult Gideon replied that on his return he would halt at Succoth and tear the backs of its elders *'with desert thorn and briar'*. It was an ancient custom, we are informed, which had still continued in use for some time on the plains of Moab.

A little further on, at the Israelite city of Penuel (near the ford where Jacob had made his mysterious crossing of the Jabbok by night), Gideon again made his request for food, only to receive the same negative answer as before. 'Very well,' replied Gideon, 'the conversation shall be continued later.'

Soon Gideon came up with the enemy and totally destroyed their army. With his own hand he put their two leaders to death. On the return journey he had several accounts to settle. First there were the citizens of Penuel; in revenge for the cold reception that he had received Gideon slaughtered the townsmen. With the elders of Succoth he confined himself to beating them with desert briars. All this hardly seemed the best way to encourage the unity of the Israelite people.

And yet just then there were certain realists who

[5] The writer has conflated Gideon's first and second expedition. But they were very different; the enemy leaders had not the same names in the one and the other. On the other hand, in the second campaign – it was in Transjordania – Gideon was acting as an avenger. He is clearly the instrument of justice, the avenger of blood in the name of his offended clan (Judg. 8:13–21).

were well aware of the urgency of political reform: they felt that at all costs it was necessary to set up a permanent central authority capable of organising the scattered Israelite forces.

A delegation attended on Gideon: *'Rule over us,'* they said to him, *'you and your sons and your grandson, because you have rescued us from the power of Midian.'* Gideon took good care not to accept at once; on the other hand, he was ambitious enough not to refuse so attractive an offer straight off. *'It is not I who shall rule over you,'* he replied, *'nor my son; Yahweh must be your lord.'* It was a clever reply: it seemed to give satisfaction to the old nomad section of the population who imagined themselves still living in the tents of Sinai. Thus Gideon ostensibly refused to assume the official title of king for, according to Yahwistic tradition, it belonged to God alone. In recompense for his refusal Gideon, like the astute peasant that he was, made certain of a considerable personal fortune. After which, with considerable cunning he assumed openly the reality of the royal power whose various prerogatives he exercised in complete freedom. Two of them were characteristic of monarchy at this period. In the first place there was the ephod; this was probably a statue of gold set up in Gideon's personal sanctuary at Ophrah and used for purposes of divination. The second manifestation of Gideon's royal power was his harem; it must have been numerous since he had seventy sons.

The land enjoyed rest for forty years, as long as Gideon lived. . . . Gideon, son of Joash was blessed in his old age; he died and was buried in the tomb of Joash his father, at Ophrah of Abiezer.

Directly after Gideon's death the Israelites once more began to *prostitute themselves to the Baals* (that is, to worship idols) *and took Baal-berith for their god. The Israelites no longer remembered Yahweh their God, who had rescued them from all the enemies round them.*

Gideon had just died. One of his sons, Abimelech, a native of Shechem, seized the power; he, however, had no scruple in proclaiming himself king. To make certain of his crown he hastened to murder sixty-eight of his brothers; only the youngest, Jotham, managed to escape. At the head of a band of robbers Abimelech extorted money from the people, besieged cities and massacred whole populations. During the siege of Thebez, a small town about ten miles from Shechem, Abimelech was hit on the head by a millstone thrown down from the ramparts by a woman. As he was dying he summoned one of his armour bearers and said to him: *'Draw your sword and kill me, that no one may say of me, "A woman killed him".'* It was considered a disgrace in the East for a soldier to be killed by a woman. None of this was very encouraging for the Monarchist party, which with increasing insistence was demanding a king. It seemed that a new Judge was needed to deal with a political situation which once again had grown dangerous.

Jephthah, Judge in Israel (Judg. 10). **About 1100.** (See map, p. 22)

After Gideon there appeared on the scene two rather insignificant Judges, Tola and Jair. They were probably chiefs of clans who had fought on behalf of the God of Israel. We know almost nothing about them.

Following these two Judges came one who certainly did not lack firmness; on occasion he seemed almost to have too much of it. His name was Jephthah and he was Judge and then king of Gilead, an Israelite tribe of Transjordania where Moses in his time had given them authorization to settle on the fine pastureland of the eastern bank of the Jordan.

Once again we encounter the same theological sequence with four stages: sin–punishment–remorse–forgiveness. As a result a new Judge, Jephthah, was sent to Gilead. Such was the theological background; the historical setting must now be examined.

Jephthah appears as an uncouth, naïve figure, almost unacquainted with the true traditions of the Law, but a believer in Yahweh. His mother was a prostitute of Mizpah in Gilead who had a child by a married man. On his father's death his legitimate sons drove out Jephthah: '*You are to have no share in our father's inheritance,*' they said. Jephthah left the house and settled in the north of Gilead where he formed a band of brigands, good-for-nothings and outlaws who existed on brigandage and holding people to ransom. In this way Jephthah became a potential military leader.

At this time the southern part of Gilead was regularly invaded and laid waste by the Ammonites, the 'Sons of the East' again, who were inveterate plunderers. Mounted on their fast-moving camels they were able to carry out swift raids. The elders of Gilead were very anxious to find a remedy for this situation; they held a meeting at Mizpah to endeavour to find someone who would lead them into battle against the Ammonites and be ruler of Gilead.

Their thoughts turned to Jephthah, a native of the country whose exploits were on everyone's lips. A delegation of elders was sent to him, but he received them coldly: '*Was it not you who hated me and drove me out of my father's house?*' he demanded bitterly. '*Why come to me when you are in trouble?*' One of the elders acknowledged humbly the wrongs done to Jephthah; let him return generously to help his tribe, and after the victory there would be little doubt of his being made chief of Gilead.

Agreement was reached. But Jephthah distrusted these subtle jurists. He required all their promises to be ratified by the solemn oath of both parties to the agreement, and this was done in a fine ceremony, held at Mizpah itself 'in the presence of Yahweh'. If he returned alive from his expedition Jephthah was to be king of the Israelite tribes of Transjordania.

The monarchical idea, the idea of unity, was making progress.

Jephthah's first campaign was against the Ammonites or Moabites,[6] whom he defeated at Aroer (in the territory of Reuben to the east of the Dead Sea), then turned back on Minnith ('twenty towns') and pursued the enemy, who were in total disorder, as far as Abel-keramim. During one of these battles Jephthah made an unfortunate vow to Yahweh: *'If you deliver the Ammonites into my hands, then the first person to meet me from the door of my house when I return in triumph from fighting the Ammonites shall belong to Yahweh, and I will offer him up as a holocaust.'* Obviously, Jephthah on returning to his native city had no scruple in putting to death one of his compatriots who had formerly sent him into exile. A vow of this kind was an authentic Canaanite practice; in these idolatrous circles human sacrifices still held an important place, and not only new-born babies were offered to the deity but also adults, as is shown by Jephthah's vow. It is

[6] The text is not very clear as two traditions are combined in it; Jephthah seems sometimes to have been concerned with the Ammonites and sometimes with the Moabites.

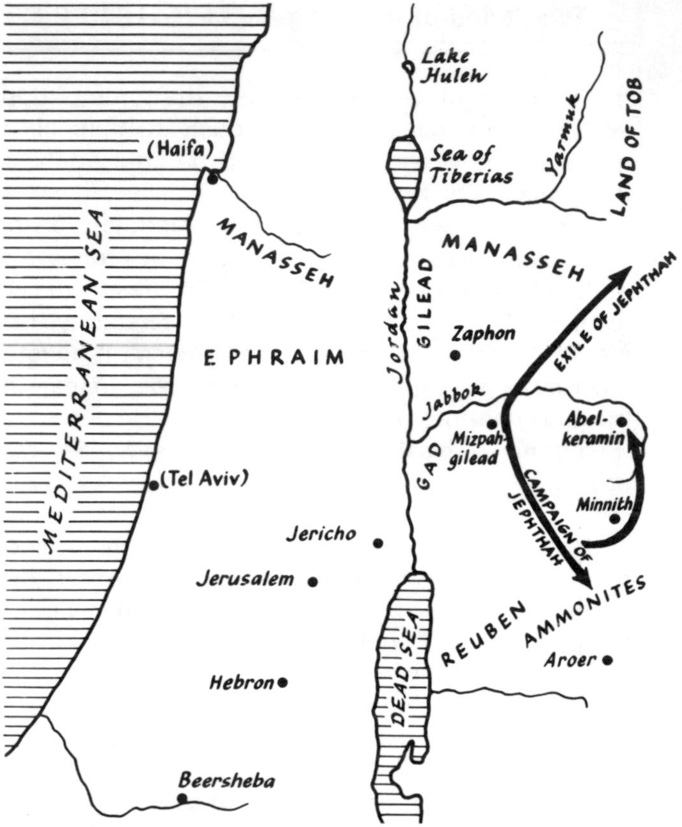

JEPHTHAH'S CAMPAIGN AGAINST THE AMMONITES AND OTHER NOMADS

It should be noticed that this campaign took place to the east of the Jordan (Transjordania).

Mizpah in Gilead: Jephthah's native city from which he was driven out by his compatriots; he sought asylum in the land of Tob. Jephthah was recalled to Mizpah by the elders of the city who came to ask the exile to deliver them from the continuing raids of the Ammonites.

Jephthah's campaign against the Ammonites (and probably also against other nomad brigands). His victories at Aroer, Minnith, Abel-keramim.

Return to Mizpah where he performs his vow (sacrifice of his daughter).

At Zaphon Jephthah settled accounts with the Ephraimites who had sought a quarrel with him.

hardly necessary to point out in passing that such a vow was directly contrary both to the letter and to the spirit of the Mosaic Law, 'Thou shalt not kill'.

Jephthah, a rough unlettered soldier although a follower of Yahweh, had little knowledge of the spiritual religion whose moral laws had been promulgated on Sinai. The local Levites seemed no better informed. In addition, of course, like all his contemporaries, he believed that he was formally bound by a vow which was irrevocable.

The rest of the story is well known. On his triumphal return to Mizpah Jephthah made his way to his own house. At that moment his daughter came through the door at the head of a troop, dancing to the sound of timbrels; this was the customary procession of the virgins who, among the Israelites, thus welcomed the warrior returning victorious to his native village. Her father's sorrow was intense, but such a vow could not be commuted. Jephthah's daughter was sacrificed, and, the very height of horror and impiety, she was sacrificed to Yahweh himself.

Jephthah's first campaign had been against the common enemy of the Israelite tribes in Transjordania, the Ammonites, the brigands settled on the tablelands near by. The second campaign was against the tribe of Ephraim. We have already observed the authoritarian, boastful and proud character of the Ephraimites. They had picked a quarrel with Gideon but the astute peasant of Ophrah had managed to extricate himself. And now, directly after Jephthah's brilliant victory over the Ammonites these same Ephraimites came to threaten him and seek a further quarrel. *'Why did you go to fight the Ammonites,'* they inquired angrily, *'without asking us to go with you? We shall burn you and your house.*' Jephthah, a former brigand leader himself, was not of the same stuff as Gideon, the small farmer who threshed his wheat with his own hands. In the first place he put matters in their true light; Ephraim had indeed been summoned to fight against the Ammonites, but had not moved. He explained that he had been obliged to go to war alone and now, he concluded, '*you come to demand an explanation from me!*' Without more ado Ephraim invaded from the other side of the Jordan. The army was concentrated at Zaphon, to the north of the Jabbok. Jephthah accepted the challenge, marched against the enemy, inflicted heavy losses and routed them completely. In utter disorder the Ephraimites who had escaped being killed endeavoured to cross over to the right bank of the Jordan. But Jephthah's men were waiting for them at the fords, and there they were killed without mercy. The Israelites, killing each other in civil war, were now even further away from unity. Jephthah reigned for six years, but always on the other side of the Jordan. It was an attempt at monarchy which had no future.

Samson the giant and popular hero (Judg. 13). **About 1075 B.C.** (See map, p. 26)

There were three judges after Jephthah; to each of them the Bible devotes only some three to five lines. They were Ibzan, Elon and Abdon, leading men who by their example helped to keep Yahwism alive.

We now come to a very strongly marked personality, Samson, the popular hero of independence, the brave giant endowed with extraordinary strength. With obvious satisfaction the writer recounts for us the adventures of this strong man in a sequence of anecdotes full of fanciful incident. The morality of some of the stories is a little doubtful on occasion and the historian feels bound to regard certain features, which are obvious additions, with considerable reservations. Nevertheless, the chapter devoted to Samson is certainly the most picturesque in the Book of Judges and this explains its popularity.

Samson in fact conducted a personal war against the Philistines, the hated enemies who had only settled recently in the land of Canaan and constituted an obvious danger for the political future of the Israelites. Samson continually set traps for them; sometimes he played outrageous tricks on them, at other times he killed great numbers of them. Since the Israelites could not be victorious on the field of battle they consoled themselves by covering the Philistines with ridicule. In this way, popular stories about Samson, which were passed from mouth to mouth and told repeatedly among the small clans in the south constituted a continual call to resistance.

The theme of these racy pages was the struggle of a national hero against the Philistines, a new people who had arrived in the Near East. They have not so far been mentioned here.[7] Since these people played a considerable role in the history of Israel something must now be said about them.

The Philistines were Indo-Europeans. A little more than a century before the events here concerning us an Aryan group, migrating slowly from the remote tablelands of upper Asia, penetrated with its chariots into Europe by way of the Balkans. These peoples had settled in the islands of the Aegean Sea and in the coastal provinces of the peninsula which at a later date was named Greece. During the upheaval caused by

[7] The name Philistine was used by the writer of Judges in the chapter concerning Jephthah when enumerating the peoples who were Israel's enemies. But many biblical scholars consider that these lists were revised at a late date and so they cannot be taken as an historical reference.

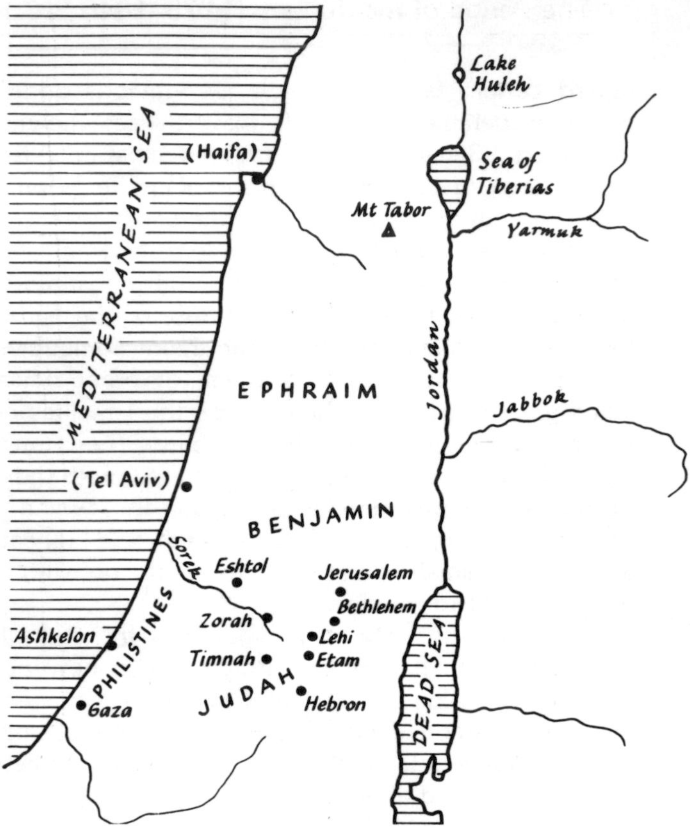

THE FIELD OF ACTION OF SAMSON.
THE POPULAR HERO (about 1075)

The preceding campaigns of the Judges (those, at least so far examined in this book) took place either in the north (Deborah) or in the central part of the country (Gideon, Jephthah).

The picturesque adventures of Samson occurred in the south, in Judah and Philistia.

Samson: born at Zorah; 'Philistine marriage' at Timnah; journey to Ashkelon where he killed thirty Philistines.

Samson at the cave of Etam. The Philistines penetrate into Judah, settle at Lehi. Anecdote of the jawbone of an ass (Ramath-lehi).

Anecdote of Gaza. Samson and the gates of the city.

Delilah of the Vale of Sorek. Capture of Samson, his death at Gaza.

the invasion of this part of the world there took place the celebrated expedition against the Aegean citadel of Troy.

Towards the middle of the twelfth century occurred a second wave of Aryans, following very nearly the same route as the first. To obtain a favourable place in which to settle the new arrivals drove out those who had previously settled in the Aegean. In these circumstances there was thus a huge mass of Aryan people obliged to depart hastily from Greece and the islands and to seek fresh territory in which to settle. They turned towards the delta of the Nile whose agricultural wealth was proverbial.

At the end of the thirteenth century the Aryans (the Egyptians gave them the name of 'Peoples of the Sea') attacked the mouth of the Nile from the west, that is, through Libya. Rameses III (1197–1165) inflicted a severe defeat on them and threw them back. In 1190 they attacked again, this time from the east of the Delta. Once more Rameses repulsed them. The Philistines, as we call them, then turned towards objectives which were less well defended; they settled to the south of Canaan in the rich plains of Sharon and, especially, of Shephelah, hitherto occupied by various Semitic tribes. The new masters of the territory quickly set up a kind of political federation. There were five kingdoms: Gaza, Gath, Ashdod, Ashkelon, and Ekron. On the other hand, the Zekals, their brothers in arms, settled in the region of Carmel.

For Israel the situation was an anxious one. The Philistines, who suddenly appeared on the scene early in the twelfth century (about 1190) were far more dangerous opponents than the native Canaanites and far more formidable than the nomad brigands of Transjordania, the Ammonites, Moabites and Edomites.

The Philistines were imperialists and within a short space they intended to annex the whole of the region situated between the wilderness of Negeb (to the south) and Lake Tiberias (to the north).[8] Now the Israelites, too, intended to possess this region, which they considered as their own property. The conflict was not long in coming. The story of Samson shows us the first engagements in this relentless struggle.

The Israelite tribes were still at a primitive stage of political development, but it did not prevent their realizing to the full what was at stake. It was a question of life or death. By making their theme a village epic, part dramatic, part amusing – namely the story of Samson – the Israelite story-tellers endeavoured to uphold the morale of their co-religionists. The national hero is intended at every turn of the story to remind the audience of the presence of the terrible Philistine danger.

From the point of view of the liberation of the Israelites Samson could not be placed on an equal footing with Gideon or Jephthah. His role, more literary than effective, consisted of maintaining among the followers of Yahweh the spirit of revenge against the 'uncircumcised' Philistines, with whom it was important not to come to terms on any pretext whatever. So we have this series of incidents filled out with more or less humorous asides.

[8] The name Palestine or Philistia means land of the Philistines. These Philistines were a strange mixture of Indo-Europeans and Aegeans (the latter being, it should be noticed, neither Semites nor Indo-Europeans) who on their journey westwards had made a more or less long halt on Crete. It was the southern coast of Canaan, where the Philistines originally settled, which was first called Philistia. That was logical enough. But later on, by some strange confusion, the land of Canaan, which had become the land of Israel, was given the name of Palestine. Thus through the mistake of ill-informed geographers the Israelites owed to the Philistines, their implacable enemies, the official name of the Promised Land.

The stories about women were cleverly exploited, as was proper in a popular narrative. Samson was betrayed by the woman whom he wished to take as his wife from among the Philistines, so he slew thirty of the uncircumcised and, full of wrath, returned to his father's house. One day he had the idea of visiting the woman who had laughed at him: he found her married to another man. In revenge for this supposed affront Sampson captured three hundred foxes, and tying them tail to tail put a lighted torch between each pair of tails. He then let them loose in the Philistines' cornfields.

These were good stories; they provoked the admiration of the Israelites and consoled them a little for the advantages continually being gained by their opponents. Then there was the jawbone of an ass which Samson picked up on the town rubbish heap. With this improvised club and alone against a great multitude Samson slew a thousand of them. As he felt very thirsty after this exploit Yahweh caused a spring of water to burst forth. All this was calculated to breed enthusiasm. Soon afterwards we come to the episode at Gaza. In this city of the Philistine confederation Samson had visited a prostitute. Hearing of this the Philistines at once planned to seize their enemy; for this purpose the gates of the city were closed. The next morning Samson found the way barred when he tried to leave. Thereupon, he calmly unhinged the gates, tore up the posts, hoisted them on his back and made his way towards Hebron.

Lastly, there was the episode of Delilah – her name means 'informer' or 'spy'. The Philistine chiefs had promised her eleven hundred silver shekels as the price of her betrayal. Samson, treacherously implored by his lover to reveal to her the secret of his great strength, in the end gave her the desired explanation. From the time of his birth, he told her, he had been a 'nazir', that is, he was consecrated to God by his mother. In accordance with the custom of the nazirs he kept all his hair: *'A razor has never touched my head . . . If my head were shorn, then my power would leave me and I should lose my strength and become like any other man.'* So Delilah had discovered what she had been asked to find out.

While Samson was asleep Delilah summoned one of her accomplices who sheared the seven locks off his head. Philistines, who were waiting in the next room, then fell upon Samson, and he could offer them no resistance. He was chained up and his eyes were put out; they then put him to turn the mill in the prison.

The great joy of the Philistines may be imagined. A little later, during a ceremony in the temple of Dagon, the chiefs of the Philistines ordered Samson to be brought before them: *'Send Samson out to amuse us,'* they said. The Philistines had no idea (the Israelite story-teller appears to have been determined to portray them as almost simple-minded) that since Samson's hair had grown again he would have recovered his former great strength. The rest of the story is well known. Samson asked the boy who was leading him to take him where he could touch the central pillars supporting the heavy roof of the building. With one great effort, exerted by pushing his arms outwards, he managed to bring down these two great masses of masonry. *'May I die with the Philistines!'* he cried. The whole building fell down on the chiefs and on the people filling the sanctuary of the god. It was a fine story whose popularity among the Israelites cannot be doubted. But they were still at too primitive a stage of development to appreciate the great moral lesson which emerged from the story of their hero. They did not understand clearly that Samson's prodigious strength

'Listen, you kings! Give ear you princes!
From me, from me comes a song for Yahweh.
I will glorify Yahweh, God of Israel . . .

'Then Israel marched down to the gates;
Yahweh's people, like heroes, . . .

'So perish all your enemies, Yahweh!
And let those who love you be like the sun
When he arises in all his strength.'

Judges 5

was merely a physical gift given by God. His hair, which he was obliged to wear long as a nazir, had nothing to do with his superhuman strength. His long hair was only the external sign of his consecrated state, just as nowadays, a monk's tonsure is. That Samson lost his strength is explained by the fact that, gradually, he was false to his nazirite vow. That later, in prison, he grew as strong as he had been previously was the result of contrition, prayer and penance. That is the moral lesson that the writer wished to emphasize: in a time of trial it is only return to God that is effective.

Deborah's period as Judge amounts to an attempt at union of the Israelite tribes of the north and south against danger from within the country, that is, the Canaanite power.

With Gideon and Jephthah it was two short-lived sovereignties which attempted in vain to rally the tribes in the north against a foreign enemy, the Midianites, Moabites and Ammonites, the nomad brigands of Transjordania.

With Samson we have a wholly different conception in the form of a fable: Israel must not forget that it must fight with all its strength and on all occasions against the Philistines, the new and formidable enemy from beyond the seas. In this way, therefore, Samson took his place, in his own rather special way, in the list of authentic Judges.

It was not very clear at the time where all these isolated, unco-ordinated actions were to lead. Fortunately, the Israelites soon came to understand that their independence, and indeed their very existence, could only be assured by achieving unity under the command of a single leader. And so we witness the appearance of the prophet Samuel, Yahweh's energetic spokesman.

Endowed with uncommon spiritual strength, and in somewhat picturesque circumstances, he was to perform the anointing of Saul and David, the first two kings of Israel.

2

TOWARDS A KING: SAMUEL

Should Samuel be regarded merely as the last of the Judges or did he have a new and more positive function? It is not easy to decide, for two distinct traditions have been woven together by the author of the First Book of Samuel. One of these traditions depicts Samuel as a prophet who attempted to solve the national and religious problem: he realized that Israel could only be saved by uniting the Twelve Tribes under a single head. In this view he served as the thread of gold linking the anarchic period of the Judges with the strongly organized and unifying epoch of the kings. He was therefore the founder of the monarchy, for although in some respects he did not favour that institution, he did in fact anoint the first two kings of Israel.

Samuel was a priest (but not a Levite) of Shiloh, the place where the Ark of the Alliance was kept. So it is to Shiloh that we must turn for the beginning of the events which follow.

Shiloh: Israel's principal sanctuary

At the end of the period of the Judges (about 1040) the Twelve Tribes were far from occupying the whole of the Promised Land, as the Israelites of the time of Moses, on coming from Sinai might well have hoped to do. In fact the various tribes of Israel were divided into four main groups separated from each other by alien communities (see map, p. xviii).

In the mountainous central region, Ephraim and Benjamin were established, flanked on the north by Manasseh and Issachar, and on the west by Dan.

In the north, were Zebulun, Asher and Naphtali, separated from the tribes in the centre by the plain of Jezreel, inhabited by Canaanites and Zekals (Peoples of the Sea).

In the south, to the west of the Dead Sea, Judah and Simeon had great difficulty in keeping in touch with the other tribes, owing to the strong barrier formed by the Jebusites (Canaanites) with their citadel of Urushalim (Jerusalem).

Finally, on the left bank of the Jordan, two tribes (or rather, two tribes and a half) stayed in Transjordania: Reuben, on the east of the Dead Sea; Gad, in the Jabbok region; and half of the important tribe of Manasseh which dwelt on both banks of the river.

These Twelve Tribes, so dangerously isolated, had so far failed to restrain the petty ambitions of their leaders, their jealous antagonisms, or the obstinate selfishness of the great families. However, the work done by the Judges, though spasmodic and disorganized must not be regarded as completely useless. The unity of the twelve tribes was brought about not by the danger from the Canaanites but by that from the Philistines.

At this time the Ark was kept in the little village of Shiloh on the heights of Ephraim between Bethel and Shechem, midway, therefore between the tribes of the north and those of the south. In the period immediately following the entry of the Hebrews into the Promised Land, Joshua had installed the Ark in this place, which thus became Israel's central, and indeed its only sanctuary. When Samuel began his career, the Ark was no longer within the enclosure of a mere tent; a kind of temple (*hekal*) – no doubt of simple structure – had been built around it. It was here, on feast days, that the tribes assembled in order *to seek Yahweh's face*, to renew their oath of fidelity to him, and also of course to settle matters of policy. Whatever its concerns, the Yahwist confederation had never forgotten Shiloh; it remained the centre and the symbol of the whole of Israel. But it is chiefly after Samson, with Eli and Samuel, that the dynamic and constructive action of this religious capital in Israel's history can be observed.

Eli, the High Priest, the custodian of the Ark in Shiloh

The sanctuary of Shiloh was served by a body of priests with a high priest at their head whose position seems to have been hereditary. At this time the office was held by Eli. He had two sons who took an active part in the worship: Hophni (in Egyptian: 'Little fish', or 'frog') and Phinehas (the Dark Skinned, the Nubian); they were far from praiseworthy, and their conduct was a source of scandal to Yahweh's worshippers.

One day a woman named Hannah came on pilgrimage. Her husband was Elkanah, an Ephraimite. She was much distressed because she had long been barren, and she besought God constantly to grant her a child. In the end, she made a vow that if her prayer was heard she would give her son to the Lord as a nazir, thus consecrating him to the service of the sanctuary. In due course, Hannah had a child whom she named Samuel (Shemu'El: heard by God). Some years later we find him at Shiloh with Eli: there *the boy went on growing in stature and in favour both with Yahweh and with men* (1 Sam. 2: 26).

Eli was a saintly man; but with age he had grown feeble and blind. He was quite aware of his sons' behaviour: they openly disregarded the rules of worship and treated the pilgrims to Shiloh with contempt. The aged priest behaved very weakly towards his sons, but, fortunately he had the young Samuel with him, and the lad's earnest devotion filled the visitors to the sanctuary with admiration.

As high priest and custodian of the Ark, Eli had attracted an active group of the best men in Israel, those who placed their hopes in Yahweh and in him alone. And scattered among the tribes many persons revered the two servants of God, Eli, almost a centenarian, and Samuel the youthful nazir, so unlike in appearance, so similar in their spiritual stature.

Moreover, in a series of revelations, Yahweh seemed to have chosen Samuel as his prophet, his spokesman, the one commissioned to transmit his message to his people, and, at times, even to reveal the future.

Hope revived in Israel: the military ambition prevalent under the Judges began to change to faith in Yahweh, who alone could shoulder the human burden and so liberate the tribes and secure the effective possession of the Promised Land.

A national catastrophe: the Ark captured by the Philistines

The Philistines were growing steadily bolder, and untiringly pursued their policy of methodical occupation of the whole land. At Aphek, where the Jaffa river rises, Israel engaged this formidable enemy in battle; the Israelites were defeated and put to flight, leaving great numbers of dead on the field.

Revenge was imperative; this time the Israelites were determined that everything should be in their favour.

They decided to have the Ark with them in the midst of their troops. Yahweh among his people could not fail to secure victory. After all, in the days of Moses and Joshua, it was under this divine protection that the Israelite armies had marched.

Accordingly, the Ark was fetched from its sanctuary in Shiloh. Hophni and Phinehas, Eli's two sons, themselves carried the Ark of *Yahweh Sabaoth, he who is seated on the cherubs*. As soon as it reached the Hebrew camp, a great welcoming shout went up, the famous *terua'ah*, that was both a war cry and a religious acclamation. The Philistines, roused by this clamour, and warned probably by their spies, were alarmed by this new factor that threatened the outcome of the conflict. 'Their God,' they said, 'has come to the camp. He is powerful; who will save us from him?' But the Philistines were brave, and besides they had their own gods to protect them. They seemed decided to fight mercilessly and to give no quarter.

For Israel this was one of the darkest days of its history; they were outwitted; the enemy thronged around them and slaughtered them, and as the climax of misfortune, the Ark was captured by the 'uncircumcised' who took the trophy to Ashdod and put it in the temple of their god Dagon.

At Shiloh, Eli, old and blind, had been placed on his seat beside the gate of the sanctuary, anxiously awaiting the messenger from the battlefield. The leaders of Israel had dispatched a Benjaminite, and as was the custom with the bearers of bad news, his clothes were torn and dust was on his head. As he raced along the streets the people quickly guessed what he had to say, and *cries filled the town*. The clamour disturbed Eli, but he soon realised its meaning. The messenger reached him and said breathlessly: *'I have come from the camp*

. . . *Israel has fled before the Philistines; the army has been utterly routed. What is worse, your two sons are dead and the Ark of God has been captured*'. *When he mentioned the Ark of God, Eli fell backward off his seat by the gate; his neck was broken and he died, for he was* (ninety-eight years) *old and heavy*.

The Philistines were filled with joy; the Israelites had been defeated and their God was a 'captive' in Ashdod. But it was a short-lived triumph; an epidemic (difficult to define) broke out in the city in which the Ark had been deposited. It was decided to remove it to Gath, another of the Five Cities, but the same scourge broke out there also. Its inhabitants speedily rid themselves of this frightening trophy and it was removed to Ekron, another capital of the Philistine confederation. The people here protested forcibly against the unwelcome guest, for as soon as it arrived they were afflicted with a grave and mysterious sickness. In the end, the priests of Dagon felt that the best solution was to return this Ark, of such alarming power, to Israel. In addition, in order to appease the wrath of the God of the Hebrews, golden objects symbolizing the disease that had struck the cities were sent with it. The chiefs of the Philistines, probably ashamed of this adventure, took this protector of Israel back to its rightful owners on a cart drawn by two milch cows. It had been held captive for seven months.

The restitution was effected at Beth-shemesh on the frontier. The farmers there were reaping the corn in the plain. Summoned in haste, the Levites took the Ark from the cart, and at once prepared a sacrifice of thanksgiving. The cows that had drawn the cart were killed and burnt as a holocaust, and the cart was cut up as firewood.

The Ark was not taken back to Shiloh; in fact that

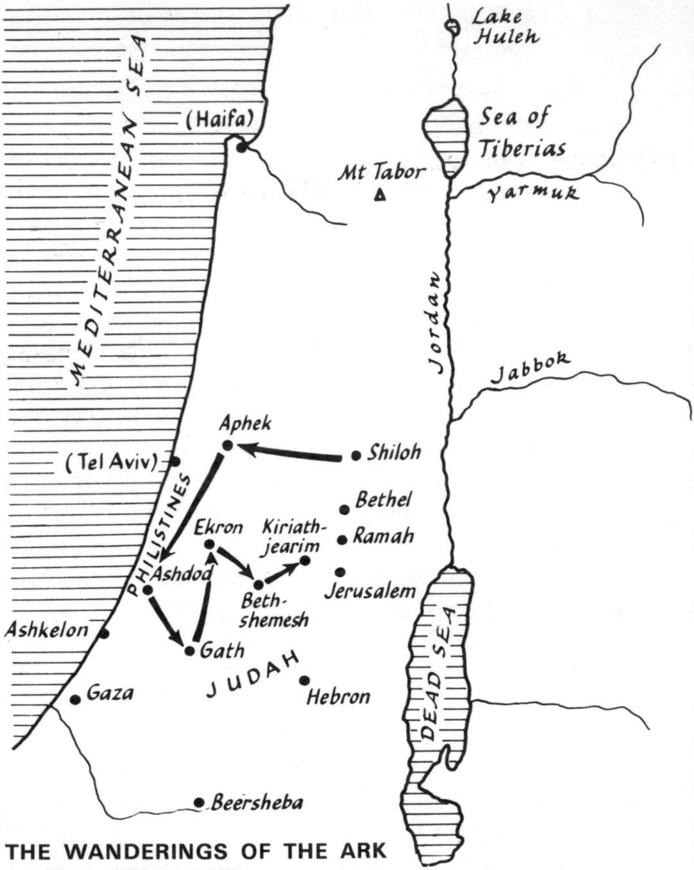

THE WANDERINGS OF THE ARK OF THE COVENANT

It was kept in the Israelite sanctuary of Shiloh.

Before the battle of Aphek, which the Israelites fought against the Philistines, the Ark was carried on to the battle-field. The Israelites were defeated and the Philistines captured the Ark.

The Ark of the Covenant was held by the Philistines: At Ashdod (in the temple of Dagon); at Gath; then at Ekron. The terrible epidemics which occurred in the cities where the Ark was, finally caused the Philistines to return it to the Israelites. Its captivity lasted seven months. Returned to the Israelites at Beth-shemesh, it was taken by the Levites to Kiriath-jearim. It was here that David was to come one day to fetch it (in about 1000 B.C.) to take it to Jerusalem, the new capital of his kingdom.

city and its sanctuary had probably been destroyed in the recent campaign (Jer. 7: 12–14). Instead, it was set up in Beth-shemesh, and soon afterwards, for reasons difficult to determine, it was taken to Kiriath-jearim (now Tel el-Azhar, west of Jerusalem). There it was placed in the house of Abinadab whose son Eleazar (though not a Levite) was appointed its guardian. It remained there until David came to take it, with great pomp, to Jerusalem. (This curious ceremony is described in a later chapter of this book.)

Samuel, the nazir of Shiloh, becomes Judge in Israel

The political and religious position of the Twelve Tribes certainly seemed to show little improvement. For twenty years, says the Book of Samuel, *the whole House of Israel longed for Yahweh* (1 Sam. 7: 2). Disorder and misfortune continued.

When Eli died and the Ark was captured, Samuel must have been very young. But this extraordinary person was not slow in displaying an intense and original activity. It was not directed mainly to war, but to breathing new spiritual strength into Israel. During the immediate time of trial Samuel was tireless in his efforts to refresh those whose courage was failing. He reminded everyone of the religious ideal that alone could save Israel from the fearful dangers that were present everywhere, and he thundered endlessly against the Baals and Astartes which Israel had begun to worship in one place or another.

Samuel was judge over Israel (1 Sam. 7: 15).

This is true, but he had nothing in common with the specifically military liberators of earlier days. We must be careful not to compare him with Deborah, the warrior poetess, and still less with the formidable brigands Gideon and Jephthah. He was also quite unlike Samson, the popular hero. It is true that on occasion Samuel led the people in battle and won some success in wars. But the vocation of this former nazir of Shiloh and custodian of the Ark was not to war. He stands out pre-eminently as a prophet, a man of God, whose purpose was to give Israel back its soul by directing its leaders to return to the path of authentic and integral Yahwism.

The Judges before Samuel are described as energetic political leaders, but their religion seems to have been sometimes rather vague. Samuel, on the contrary, believed that the people's salvation lay solely in whole-hearted obedience to God. His faith was of the kind that moves mountains.

And so we find this new type of Judge becoming an itinerant priest, travelling from one sanctuary to another, making regular visits to the various places of pilgrimage. He offered the sacrifice, addressed the crowds, and continually exhorted them to return to their God. He told the people that they would soon be delivered, provided they realized how deeply they had failed to keep the Law of Moses. Every year he went *on circuit* (1 Sam. 7: 16) – a strange biblical expression – through the main religious centres, Bethel, Gilgal, Mizpah, bringing consolation to the People of God in words calculated to revive the religion of Yahweh that had grown cold. Finally he returned to his native town of Ramah,[1] for his home was there; there too he judged Israel. *And there he built an altar to Yahweh.*

[1] Ramah: probably the present village of er-Ram, seven miles north of Jerusalem.

A turning-point in Israel's history: the Chosen People demand a king (About 1030)

At this period, all the great nations of the Middle East had at their head a king who was the symbol of their national pride and the centre of their life. Why were the Hebrews so long in adopting the monarchic system? Examples of it were all around them, and yet since the earliest days of the Judges they had hesitated. In fact, the matter was somewhat more complicated.

First of all, Israel, as a State in process of formation, obviously needed a *king*, or at least a permanent Judge, ensuring a single military command as well as a collective policy for the Twelve Tribes. A military leader was essential. Secondly, Israel, as the People of God, also needed a priest or a prophet at the head of their organization, some inspired personality with the power to lead them along the road to God. This was the institutional drama of Israelite theocracy. Where then was the man to be found fit to be both king of men and man of God?

When Samuel became judge – a political and religious leader, who was more political than religious – it was reasonable to suppose that the problem had to some extent been solved. But Samuel was growing old. His two sons, whom he had made local 'judges' in Beersheba, were hardly fitted to succeed him. Action was imperative before Samuel's death. Since the tribes of Israel still had him with them as their powerful intercessor inspired by Yahweh it seemed obvious that he should be asked to appoint his own successor before his death. The elders therefore came together and said, in words that must have been somewhat painful to him: '*Look, you are old and your sons do not follow your ways. So give us a king to rule over us . . .*' that is, someone to control the political and military government of Israel. There followed a keen and lengthy discussion, both political and theological, between Samuel and those who advocated monarchy. Very possibly the biblical writer has here given in dialogue form the two opposing views then current among the tribal leaders. And later events have certainly coloured the account.

There was, in fact, a monarchist party, and this was in the majority. With some good show of reason, these men held that Israel's existence was in imminent danger. Disaster could only be avoided by the immediate institution of kingship. On the other hand, a forceful minority, headed by Samuel, stood for the old nomadic ideal. Yahweh was the protector, the God whom Israel must absolutely trust. The people should be exact in their observance of the Law, and each tribe was to enjoy freedom obeying merely its own leaders.

It had to be either monarchy or theocracy. Israel was at the cross-roads. The choice was inescapable.

'*Let us have a king to rule over us . . . like the other nations*' (1 Sam. 8: 6). These were the words addressed by the tribal leaders to Samuel. He replied sharply that Israel was not like other nations; it was unique; its essentially religious destiny could not be assured and carried out by a secular government. Israel's sovereign was Yahweh himself.

The discussion was useless. Samuel was well aware that the elders had their minds made up. In desperation he appealed to Yahweh, who answered: '*It is not you they have rejected; they have rejected me from ruling over them . . . Obey their voice; only, you must warn them solemnly and instruct them in the rights of the king who is to reign over them.*'

In the outcome, the minority (represented in Scripture

by Samuel) gave way to the pressure of numbers, although they were careful to emphasize the disadvantages of kingship. The political innovators were forewarned of the political disillusion awaiting them. They wanted a king: they should have one: but they would be sorry for it. The king *'will take your sons and assign them to his chariotry and his cavalry, and they will run in front of the chariot. He will use them as leaders of a thousand and leaders of fifty* (subdivisions of the army: which was divided into groups of 10, 50, 100, and 1000); *he will make them plough his ploughland and harvest his harvest and make his weapons of war and the gear for his chariots. He will also take your daughters as perfumers, cooks and bakers. He will take the best of your fields, of your vineyards and olive groves and give them to his officials. . . . He will tithe your flocks and you yourselves will become his slaves. When that day comes, you will cry out on account of the king you have chosen for yourselves, but on that day God will not answer you'* (1 Sam. 8: 11–18). (These misfortunes were, in fact, realized during Solomon's reign.)

Samuel was talking to the deaf; the people refused to listen to him, and said: *'No! We want a king so that we in our turn can be like the other nations; our king shall rule* (that is, administer) *us and be our leader and fight our battles.'* Yahweh, therefore, commanded Samuel: *'Obey their voice and give them a king.'* The monarchists had won; the theocratic party was defeated.

So Samuel now awaited the moment when God would point out to him the man who was to be the first king of Israel.

3

SAUL: THE FIRST KING OF ISRAEL (1030–1010)

At last, after a period of indecision and hesitation (the period of the Judges) a real king, worthy of the name, uniting practically all Israel under his rule, appeared in the annals of the Chosen People. His name was Saul.

This experience of kingship began excellently: it ended very badly. Fortunately, David, the little herdsman of Bethlehem, was at hand to take up the royal inheritance and ensure its prosperity.

The quest for the lost she-donkeys

At the time when the elders were persistently asking Samuel to find them a king, the family of Kish, a man of quality, lived at Geba[1] in the territory of the tribe of Benjamin. One of his sons, Saul (Sha 'ul = asked of God), was, we are told, extremely handsome and of exceptional stature.

One morning Kish noticed that some of his she-donkeys were missing. It should be realized that in those farms of Canaan the cattle were not enclosed. Donkeys, in particular, were semi-free; when they

1 Three miles north of Jerusalem. Now Tel el-Ful in the Wadi Fara. American excavations, 1922.

were needed for transport they had to be rounded up in the fields. If, by chance, they had wandered off, they were easily found, because each of them was branded with its owner's mark. This time, however, Kish could not discover them. He therefore told his son Saul and one of his slaves to go in search of them. After three fruitless days, Saul, fearing that his father would be anxious on account of their long absence, decided to go back to the farm. But the slave suggested that they should carry on at least as far as the neighbouring town of Ramah, for a *man of God* lived there, well known as a seer, and he might be able to indicate the exact spot where the animals had fled. Saul hesitated; there was no food left, and he had no money to pay for the consultation. But the slave had shown more forethought and had brought a little money with him – a quarter of a silver shekel (roughly, ten shillings) – enough to settle the seer's account.

Surprising as it may seem, it was Samuel, one of Israel's Judges, the restorer of the religion of Yahweh, the saviour of the Law, who was this local seer, able, in return for an offering, to find lost property, strayed animals, and so forth.

Saul and the slave therefore went to look for him. Passers-by told them that the seer was on the point of leaving the city to bless a sacrifice at a neighbouring high-place. If they hurried, they would probably find him there. At the entrance to the city the travellers said to one of the men about the place: *'Tell me, please, where the seer's house is?'* This man was Samuel himself, and he answered: *'I am the seer'*. He examined closely the athletic young man whose arrival had been made known to him in a vision the night before. He was well aware of Yahweh's plans for this stranger.

Without disclosing his mission, Samuel welcomed

the young Benjaminite heartily. He led him to the sacrificial meal, which he himself was about to attend, and he told the cook to set before the lad the leg and the tail, the choice portions that were reserved for an honoured guest. He kept his eyes on him; there could be no doubt that this was the person whom Yahweh had appointed to be the saviour of the Chosen People.

That evening Samuel took Saul into his own house, and gave him the place on the house-top where a blanket was spread out for travellers.

Saul is consecrated

Saul was still concerned about his father's donkeys, but Samuel had other ideas. In the morning, at the break of day, the seer awakened his guest, led him through the gate of the city and went a short way with him. There then occurred a curious incident. *Samuel said to Saul: 'Tell the servant to go ahead of us, but you stand still for a moment and I shall make known to you the word of God.' Then Samuel took a phial of oil and poured it on Saul's head; then he kissed him, saying, 'Has not Yahweh annointed you prince over his people Israel? You are the man who must rule Yahweh's people, and who must save them from the power of the enemies surrounding them.'*

The young man's surprise can be imagined. To give him confidence, Samuel foretold three events which he would witness. First, he would meet two of his father's servants who would tell him that the donkeys had been found and that they were worried about him at home. Further on, he would meet three men going up to Bethel; one would be carrying three kids; one, three loaves of bread, and the third a skin of wine. They would greet him, and he would be given two loaves. After this, on entering Gibeah, he would unexpectedly meet *'a group of prophets coming down from the high place, headed by harp, tambourine, flute and lyre; they will be in an ecstasy'* (1 Sam. 10: 5). These people belonged to a religious confraternity whose members reached an ecstatic state by means of music and gesticulation, rather like dancing dervishes. It was a part of the ancient religious practice of Canaan that the worship of Yahweh allowed for some time. It is mentioned again in the Bible.

'Then,' explained Samuel, *'the spirit of Yahweh will seize upon you, and you will go into an ecstasy with them, and be changed into another man . . . for God is with you.'* He ended by assigning a meeting place at the sacred town of Gilgal, near Jericho. *'You are to wait seven days* (a sacred number) *for me to come to you, and then I will show you what you are to do.'*

All the signs foretold to Saul occurred at the stated times and places. This put the words of the man of God beyond doubt. In addition, Saul experienced a strange inner conviction which virtually made him a new man.

As soon as he returned to Geba his father questioned him about his conversation with Samuel. Saul answered casually *'He only told us that the donkeys were already found.'*

Samuel's official designation of Saul as Israel's king (about 1030)

The choice made by Samuel very secretly on the outskirts of Ramah was indicative only. The oil he poured on the young man's head was a symbolic proclamation. Although his spiritual worth was considerable and although he had been officially entrusted with the duty of finding a king for Israel, a private religious rite of this kind was insufficient guarantee that the 'Lord's anointed' would have the powers enabling him to govern the People of God. As soon as possible, there had to be a ceremony that would be simultaneously both secular and religious. This was a characteristically Israelite custom.

In order, therefore, to designate the king in the traditional way, *Samuel called together the people* (or, more probably, the elders of the tribes) *to Yahweh at Mizpah*. There followed a divination rite to discover which tribe, clan, family and finally, which individual, God had chosen to rule over Israel. Unfortunately, the exact method used is unknown.[2] The final result was the appointment of Saul, the son of Kish. They looked for him in vain. Yahweh revealed that he was *hidden among the baggage*. So he was discovered and brought before the people, a splendid person, head and shoulders taller than them all. Samuel cried out proudly: *'Have you seen the man Yahweh has chosen? Of all the people there is none to equal him.'* And all present acclaimed the new sovereign.

This does not mean, however, that the theocratic and anti-monarchist party had given up the struggle. The verses that follow prove the contrary.

First of all, after Saul had risen to power, Samuel was at pains to give a public reminder of the people's rights and the king's duties. He drew up a kind of charter (thus indicating that the monarchy would be constitutional) which was placed *before Yahweh* (that is, probably in front of the Ark in its new abode at

[2] It may have been by means of the teraphim, material used in divination, but very little is known about it. Or it may have been the ephod, another mysterious object employed in questioning God. Or again it may have been by urim and thummim, a sacred lottery, probably equivalent to tossing a coin. All these oracles which at this remote period were regarded as intimations of God's will, were later condemned by the law of Israel as examples of witchcraft and magic. Saul's election to kingship by lot is comparable to a similar method adopted in ancient Greece (fifth to fourth centuries B.C.), for the election of magistrates and even of war ministers. It was also by lot that the apostles elected Matthias to take the place of the traitor Judas (Acts 1: 23–26).

Beth-shemesh). Various documents surviving from the ancient East indicate that at this period, in Egypt, Babylon and Canaan, treaties were deposited in the temples at the feet of a statue of a god, as a sign that the god was a witness of the contract.

Secondly, some of the people sneered openly. The elevation of this hitherto unknown young peasant to the throne only made some scroundrels scoff: '*How can this fellow save us?*' To mark their contempt some of the elders refrained from offering any gifts to the new 'King'.

The opposition, therefore, was weighty. Saul was morally obliged to perform some outstanding action without delay.

Saul's first striking victory: over the Ammonites

Saul, like the Judges before him who in between their war-like expeditions continued to look after their land, spent his time in daily work on his home farm at Gibeah.

While he was thus engaged, the Ammonites – a nomadic people from Transjordania – decided to attack. Their king, Nahash, laid seige to the Israelite city of Jabesh-gilead, on the opposite bank of the Jordan. The elders of Jabesh sent messengers to every tribe requesting help and assistance. But these were received only with tears and groans; defeatism was the general mood; the military weakness of the tribes was invoked as an excuse. At Gibeah, the people declared that they were overwhelmed by the fact that they were unable to provide the aid which the delegates from Jabesh begged; they offered sympathy, weeping and lamentation, but the beseiged could count on nothing more.

While this was happening, Saul came back with his animals from the fields. He was told how things

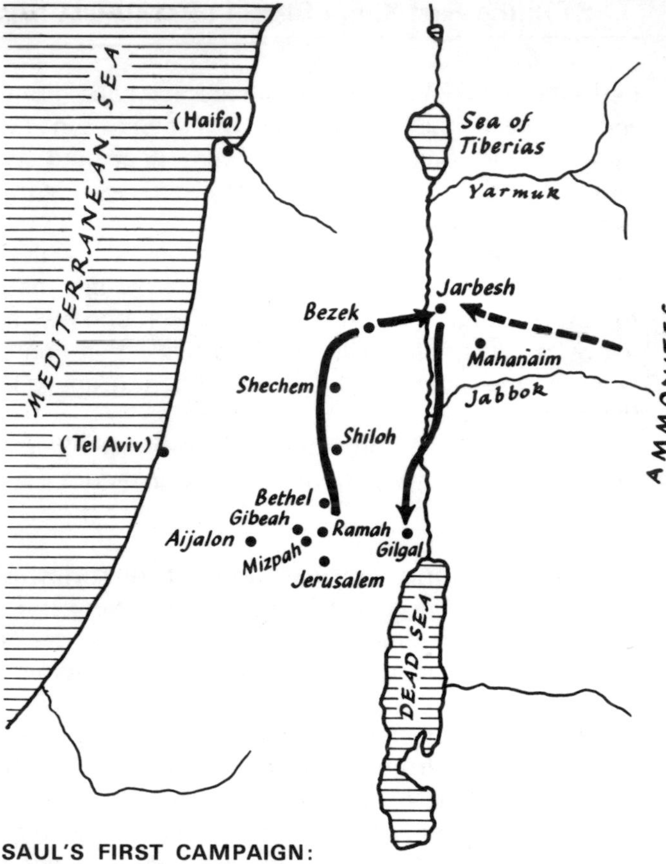

SAUL'S FIRST CAMPAIGN: AGAINST THE AMMONITES

At Ramah Samuel anointed Saul in secret.

At Mizpah Saul is chosen by lot as king of Israel. Then Saul returned to Gibeah to his farm. Warned by the inhabitants of Jabesh (in Transjordania), a city besieged by the Ammonites, Saul mobilized the warriors of the tribes; he went up to Bezek where he assembled his army; he then relieved Jabesh and cut the Ammonites in pieces. He returned by way of Gilgal where he was confirmed as king. Samuel officially gave up his judgeship.

stood. *At once the spirit of Yahweh seized on him . . . and his fury was stirred to fierce flame. He took a yoke of oxen, cut them in pieces and sent throughout the territory of Israel with these words: 'If anyone will not march with Saul, this shall be done with his oxen!'* It was a vigorous summons to resistance, but also a hidden threat to those who were trying to withdraw from their sacred and fraternal duty.

Israel's forces were mobilized in record time, for Jabesh had to be reinforced before the Ammonite attack began. Saul inspected the troops from the northern and southern tribes, (that is from Israel and Judah) at Bezek, on the direct route to Jabesh. They set out without further delay, and approached the Ammonite camp secretly. A furious battle ensued, in which Saul was the victor.

Saul's kingship is confirmed: Samuel retires as judge

Saul needed a brilliant success, and this he achieved at Jabesh. Henceforth his position was secure.

The Bible then records a curious event, difficult to interpret – Saul's second royal investiture after this Transjordanian adventure. Samuel is reported as saying: *'Let us go to Gilgal*[3] *and reaffirm the monarchy there.'* And at Gilgal, the Bible states, Saul was proclaimed king before Yahweh. And yet had he not already been king since his designation at Mizpah? In the involved passage in which the scribe, as usual, combines documents very different in character, (monarchist as well as anti-monarchist) without in any way attempting to unify them, it is sometimes difficult to be sure of the

[3] Gilgal, sometimes called Galgala, between the Jordan and Jericho. Joshua had long maintained his base camp there. It was the holy place of the tribe of Benjamin.

precise state of affairs. Possibly the anointing at Mizpah was historically the valid one; or perhaps the ceremony at Gilgal should alone be so considered. It remains an open question.

In any case, an event of considerable importance certainly occurred at Gilgal; the surrender by Samuel of his judicial function over Israel. His resignation is, of course, explicable, though strange, and it receives further explanation from later events.

He took it upon himself to declare publicly that henceforward he would not be responsible for the political future of Israel, since the Twelve Tribes now, according to their wish, had a king of their own.

He asked to be relieved of his duty. The elders made no attempt to conceal their pleasure. They showered compliments upon him; he had never failed to observe justice; his loyalty had always been above criticism; his disinterestedness was proverbial; and he had fully maintained the dignity required of his high and difficult office.

In thanking them for these kind words, Samuel repeated his warning about the dangers of monarchy. He urged them to obey their new king, but he reminded them forcibly of their duties to Yahweh.

It was a lengthy and eloquent speech, but it did not mean that he intended to become an ordinary member of the community once more. He renounced his political authority, but he meant to retain his powers as a religious leader. He did not make this standpoint clear at Gilgal, but during the reign of Saul and in the beginning of David's, he asserted his rights as a prophet, as God's mouth-piece, confronting the secular leader. There can be no doubt of his active supervision in spiritual matters, and, when necessary, he had no hesitation in speaking out loudly and clearly to the king in the name of Yahweh. This was a foreshadowing of the activity of the later prophets.

Saul's reign begins with glory: his second campaign – against the Philistines

The thirteenth and fourteenth chapters of 1 Samuel record Saul's second campaign with unconcealed pride and also with a strong emphasis on its tactical details. These confused operations took place in the very heart of Canaan.

It is at this point that Jonathan first appears on the stage of history. He stands out as an ardent soldier, a clever tactician, equal to any emergency. With it all, he remained true-hearted and most kindly. We shall meet him again by the side of the young David, whose friend and companion in arms he became.

Inspired by Saul and his son, Israel's army registered some outstanding achievements. In spite of their rudimentary equipment[4] Saul's men performed really astonishing exploits. But in all prudence they had to confine themselves to guerilla encounters and to indecisive engagements. The Philistines were defeated, but far from being crushed. Their moral setback was nevertheless considerable. For the first time they were put at a disadvantage by Israel. Still, their army, well equipped, well organized and strong in numbers managed to regain its bases in Philistia. The outcome, in fact, is best described as a stalemate.

[4] The Israelites went to the battlefield with their farm tools, since the Philistines had taken all their arms. In the Hebrew villages under Philistine control, it was forbidden to set up a forge on which swords or lances might be made. *Hence all the Israelites were in the habit of going down to the Philistines to sharpen every ploughshare, axe, mattock or goad.* We even know the cost of these repairs; *two-thirds of a shekel for ploughshares and axes, and one third for sharpening mattocks and straightening goads* (1 Sam. 13: 19–21).

The first dispute between Saul the king and Samuel the prophet

At heart, Samuel, the spokesman of the theocratic minority (the government of the Twelve Tribes by Yahweh whose will was expressed through oracles and prophets) found it difficult to admit the existence of a human king as Israel's guide and ruler. The anti-monarchist party dreamt of a return to the religiously governed economy of the desert of Sinai where God had proclaimed his own law through the mouth of Moses.

Nevertheless there was a king, and it was Samuel who had discovered, presented and consecrated him. Even so this did not prevent Samuel from considering this earthly kingship as merely a last resource. The secular sovereign must therefore be most careful not to transgress the Law, and most scrupulous in the observance of public worship. (In the ancient East such worship was immensely important; the gods demanded an exact performance of its ritual.)

Any departure from the norm was regarded as an act of disrespect to God. This was the very delicate issue on which Saul was very closely watched. He had to make but a single false move and the voice of the man of God thundered in Yahweh's name.

The first controversial matter that arose between Samuel and Saul, occurred at Gilgal. Saul had made a hurried, strategical retreat along the Jordan towards Jericho; Samuel had told him to meet him within seven days at Gilgal (1 Sam. 10: 8); for the prophet had decided that before the decisive conflict, holocausts and propitiatory sacrifices must be offered in that holy city. Saul had kept the appointment punctually, but days passed without Samuel appearing.

This involved a period of waiting which was disastrous

both psychologically and tactically. Saul's soldiers 'trembled' and deserted in their hundreds, crossing the river and scattering throughout Transjordania. He had had a powerful army, but only six hundred men were left. In addition, his position was very difficult, and open at any time to a Philistine attack. Since Samuel who should have performed the sacrifice was absent, Saul decided to offer the victims himself.

The ceremony was hardly over when Samuel appeared; Saul hurried to greet the aged priest, but his greetings were ill-received. The king tried his best to explain why he had behaved in this very understandable way. The army had begun to disband; the Philistines were threatening to attack, and Samuel had not appeared. So Saul felt it his duty to offer the holocaust himself in order to placate Yahweh before the battle.

Samuel was angry in the extreme: *'You have acted like a fool,'* he said. *'If you had carried out the order Yahweh your God commanded you, Yahweh would have confirmed your sovereignty over Israel for ever. But now your sovereignty will not last. Yahweh has searched out a man for himself after his own heart, and designated him leader of his people, since you have not carried out what Yahweh ordered you.'* This was a prophetic reference to David.

With these fearful words, Samuel left the Israelite camp.

His reaction may well appear severe. Saul's error does not seem as serious as the haughty custodian of the Law asserted. For it is a fact that at this period, the Lord's anointed was truly authorized to offer a sacrifice to Yahweh, especially when a priest who was expected, failed to arrive. The somewhat rigid line taken by the prophet may well be a covert protest against the king's political (and even religious) aims. If the adversaries of the monarchy believed that they had a puppet at their disposal whose strings could be pulled at will, they were obviously mistaken. The peasant from Gibeah whom they had invested with regal power was a man of strong character, and he meant to exercise his kingly power to the full.

In any case, his activities were in formal contradiction with the ideas of the theocratic party, of which Samuel remained to the last the untiring leader.

This, then, was the first violent dispute between these two authorities: the king and the prophet. It was not to be by any means their last. But however painful the event, it hardly seems to have affected Saul's military projects. He carried on the war, and led its operations with admirable strategy. Even so, the terrible prediction uttered by Samuel must have disturbed him very seriously, and thus, more or less consciously, prepared the way for those alarming neurotic attacks which slowly engulfed him.

Saul: a brilliant series of military successes (see map, p. 59)

Saul had checked the Philistine advance by a resounding blow. This momentary suspension of hostilities enabled the king to organize his forces on a proper military footing. To begin with, the troops were equipped with weapons other than just farm tools; swords and spears were forged in the numerous cities recently freed from Philistine occupation or control. Saul also set himself to recruit a professional army. *Any strong man or man of valour that caught Saul's eye he recruited into his service* (1 Sam. 14: 52). With a war machine of this character, it was obvious that better results could be expected than from peasants with their merely temporary recruitment.

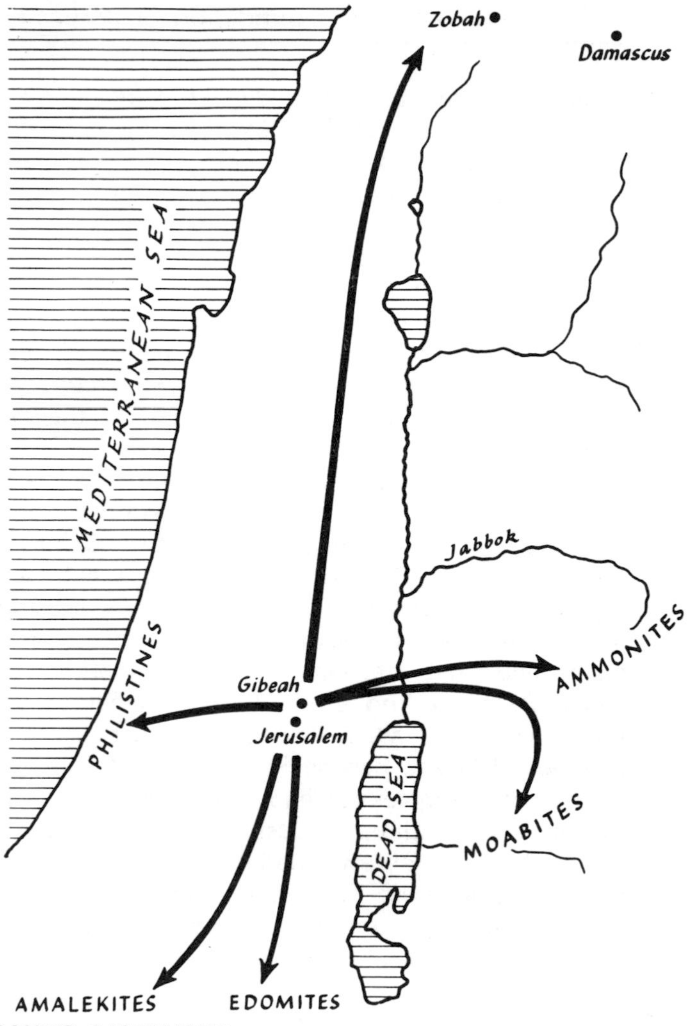

SAUL'S CAMPAIGNS

After the first campaign against the Ammonites (see map, p. 52), Saul, starting from Gibeah, his capital, was in personal charge of the following six expeditions:

1. Against the Philistines to the west.
2. Against Moab to the east.
3. Against Ammon to the east.
4. Against Edom to the south.
   Against Zobah (?) to the north.
6. Lastly, in the extreme south, against the Amalekites.

Saul soon felt able to undertake campaigns further afield. On the east of the Dead Sea, he attacked first the Ammonites and then the Moabites. He may also have attacked the Edomites on the south of this same sea – unless we are to read 'Aram', instead of Edom, on account of the mention of the Aramean fortress of Zobah in the text. In short, the warrior king made the frontiers of the Promised Land secure, those frontiers so often invaded by the 'Sons of the East', pillaging camel-drivers and relentless raiders who had regularly brought distress and misery to Canaan. In this sphere, therefore, Saul was undeniably successful.

But Israel's most hated enemies were the Amalekites, a nomad people in the far south, beyond the territory occupied by the Philistines, between Canaan and the Sinai desert. This time it involved a campaign of significant dimensions, a 'holy war', suggested or rather demanded by Samuel himself who once again maintained that he was Yahweh's spokesman. He began by reminding Saul of the criminal activity of the Amalekites: when Israel, only just beyond the confines of Egypt, had decided to take the direct route to Sinai, the Amalekites had fallen upon the troops of Moses at Rephidim, to destroy them, but had been repulsed. The Hebrews had not forgotten the trials inflicted upon them by their neighbours. Samuel continued: *'Now, go and strike down Amalek; put him under the ban* (anathema) *with all that he possesses.*[5]

[5] Amalek: the eponymous ancestor of the Amalekite tribe: their king at this period was Agag. Anathema = in Hebrew: *herem*. In remote periods, and throughout the East, this word was used to express the complete destruction by the victor, not only of the enemy people, but also of everything they owned. Before battle, and as an appeal for the tribal god's personal concern in their victory, he was promised the allotment of all the booty. Men, women and children, domestic animals and the flocks, were all slaughtered without exception. Towns and their houses were burnt and pulled down stone by stone. Only the precious metals were saved, and after purification by fire, deposited in the treasury of the god who had granted this great triumph. Naturally no personal

Do not spare him, but kill man and woman, babe and suckling, ox and sheep, camel and donkey' (1 Sam. 15: 2–3).

The prospect of a new campaign, however, was perfectly acceptable to Saul. With his troops hardened in warfare, well equipped and in good order as the result of their earlier battles, he advanced towards the south, attacked scattered encampments in the Negeb, and collected considerable booty in men and animals.

The herem was obligatory, at least in principle, because of Samuel's orders given in God's name. The soldiers, of course, interpreted it in their own way, and the Bible records how in fact it was observed. *Saul and the army spared . . . the best of the sheep and cattle, the fatlings and lambs, and all that was good. They did not want to put those under the ban; they only put under the ban what was poor and worthless.* It was an odd procedure, but probably quite common. Even so, to eastern eyes it was a sacriligious act.

Victory was complete: the Amalekites were either killed or scattered.

The second dispute between Saul and Samuel

The news travelled quickly; it was not long before Samuel learnt of the sinful liberty taken by Saul and his men with regard to the herem. This was a further religious offence on the part of the king of Israel, and Samuel was grieved and angry, *and all night long he cried out to Yahweh*. This king had been anointed by God; his every action therefore should have shown him clearly as God's servant, but he played fast and loose

looting of any kind by the soldiers was allowed: the least infringement of this sacred labour was visited by the most serious social catastrophes. During Joshua's 'conquest of the Promised Land,' we see the application of this 'herem'. But it was probably not so frequently applied as the Scriptures, with their tendency to epic exaggeration, imply.

with the sacred traditions of Yahwism and the directives of the inspired prophets.

Early in the morning Samuel set out to restore order and, as we have seen, he did not fear to use harsh measures. He reached Gilgal, where Saul and his men had assembled to offer a sacrifice of thanksgiving.

Saul had always been afraid of the prophet, and he was careful to meet him with words of welcome: '*Blessed may you be by Yahweh! I have carried out Yahweh's orders.*' Samuel treated this as impudence: '*Then what is the meaning of this bleating of sheep in my ears, and the lowing of oxen I hear?*' They were in fact the cries of the animals that had been surreptitiously withdrawn from the herem. . . . With some difficulty Saul tried to throw the blame on his soldiers; he explained that they had not yet fully completed the herem; they had in fact spared the best animals captured in the Amalekite camps, but this was only a partial postponement, for these were to be sacrificed to Yahweh on that day.

The strict Yahwistic principles of Samuel could no longer accept the spectacle of these pitiful excuses from a king who put the blame for religious wrongdoing upon the community. His reply was crushing: '*Small as you may be in your own eyes, are you not head of the tribes of Israel? Yahweh has anointed you king over Israel.*' The defence made by the accused was pitiful. It was met by the most terrifying sentence from the man who had himself consecrated Saul: '*Since you have rejected the word of Yahweh, he has rejected you as king.*'

Saul was appalled and confessed that he had sinned: '*I have sinned, for I have transgressed the order of Yahweh and your directions, being afraid of the people and doing what they said.*' It was still the same excuse;

the head laid the blame on his subordinates. Samuel, disgusted by such cowardice, made a move to leave. Saul tried to restrain him by holding on to the hem of his garment and tore it. It was an ill omen, a disturbing symbol, and Samuel was quick to make use of it: *'Today Yahweh has torn the kingdom of Israel from you and given it to a neighbour of yours who is better than you.'* (The prediction referred to David who was as yet unknown to those who heard it.)

Saul begged Samuel not to destroy his prestige in the sight of the soldiers and elders, as would be the case if he did not take part in the sacrifice then being prepared. Samuel gave his consent, but with the proviso that Agag the king of the Amalekites, so far spared from the herem, should be brought out and killed on the spot by Saul. In this way, to some extent, reparation was made for the ritual offence. Men's minds were crude, and primitive Yahwist religion was undoubtedly merciless. But it did mean that the Law of God – even though most imperfectly understood – had to be obeyed.

After the sacred meal Samuel left for Ramah. He was *very sorry* for Saul. But neither of them was to meet again.

Saul retains his kingship

After this encounter, it might logically be supposed that the king of Israel would be deprived of his throne, but nothing of the sort happened. Samuel left Gilgal after taking part in the sacrifice; the army and the elders seem to have scarcely bothered about the disagreement between their military chieftain and their religious leader. In any case, to consider matters objectively, why should there be any essential change in the way things were then organized? Saul seemed to have succeeded completely in all his undertakings. From such evidence as the historian can gather it is clear that the people were satisfied with the positive results achieved by the monarchy. We may consider, for example, the unexpected victory over the Philistines, who though certainly not destroyed, had been hurled back to their territory along the coast; the steady subjugation of the small outlying areas of Canaanite resistance that still remained; the resounding victories over external enemies which had previously constituted an ever-present threat; the advance in co-operation between the Hebrew tribes, who had never before so deeply felt the need of a fraternal alliance for the preservation of the Yahwist confederation.

All this was due to a prudent king, whose private life remained essentially simple. The monarchist party could therefore consider with some satisfaction the institution of kingship which, as we have seen, it had urged Samuel to establish.

In reality, however, the future of Israel and of the monarchy was very uncertain. First, there was the Canaanite danger. It was not so serious as in the time of Joshua. But the Amorites, who formed the core of the original population of Canaan, still held a number of towns, villages and strong places (Jerusalem, for example), and this was a serious hindrance to the territorial unity of the Hebrews.

Then there was the danger from the Philistines. Saul had indeed inflicted a serious defeat upon them, but through a tactical error he had missed the chance to crush them once for all. They had withdrawn their forces from the battlefield and were ready, when the next opportunity occurred, to take up the fight again. And though they had been driven from the heights of Ephraim, they immediately began to penetrate into the heights of Judah, in the south. In fact, they constituted an enduring threat.

In addition to all this, Saul's tactlessness revived the ancient rivalries between the Twelve Tribes. He himself belonged to the tribe of Benjamin, and rather too obviously promoted the welfare of its members. The officers of the army (commanders of a hundred or a thousand men) were all Benjaminites; and as a reward for their achievements, Saul gave them *fields and vineyards*.

Moreover, Saul's sullen and suspicious disposition became increasingly unbearable to those near him. Sometimes he was straightforward, just and sociable; at other times he gave way to fierce anger, senseless passion and fearful cruelty. He was in fact showing the first signs of that unbalanced mental state into which he was soon to fall. Even so, he remained a great king to the very end.

Samuel's terrible prophecy hastened the collapse of Saul's mind. He believed that he had sinned against Yahweh, who no longer wished him to be king and had already chosen his successor. But he hardened his heart and set himself to continue his work, even though he was inwardly convinced that his efforts, being merely human, were in vain. Therein lies the tragedy of the man. He could not imagine that he could really frustrate the divine decree, and he was always expecting the arrival of the new king who would demand the crown in God's name. Hence his fits of madness, his outbursts of rage and despair.

It may be asked why this man, chosen, elected and appointed by God as the saviour of Israel, should have so largely failed in his mission. But we should not forget that God always works through people without taking their free will from them. A choice between good and evil is always possible, and, too often, Saul chose evil.

He still continued to conduct victorious campaigns, to molest the enemy, to secure Israel's political life. But increasingly he seemed to be weighed down by his responsibilities. And in fact he achieved no lasting results in any sphere.

This was the time when a young shepherd of the tribe of Judah first appeared. His name was David.

4

SAUL AND DAVID

At the time when the unhappy Saul was beginning to experience the first attacks of that madness which was to mark the end of his reign, a young shepherd of the southern tribe of Judah was looking after the family flock near Bethlehem. He was handsome, with a face that radiated sympathy, and he was intelligent. He had fine eyes, and hair of reddish-brown – unusual characteristics in a member of an eastern community. He was of middle height, but well proportioned. His body was lithe and athletic.

His father, one of the distinguished men of Bethlehem, was called Isai, which we usually call Jesse. The young shepherd's name was David.[1]

We have already seen how hard and exhausting was a shepherd's life, alone in the vast grass-covered plains. Day and night he had to defend his flock against both thieves and wild beasts. Later on David admitted that in his youth he had fought with bears and lions[2]

[1] Etymologists have suggested that the name David means 'beloved', but some biblical scholars prefer to translate it by 'head' or 'leader'.

[2] Sam. 17: 34–37. The lion did not disappear from Palestine until the Middle Ages, at the time of the Crusades; it was the European nobility, keen hunters, who exterminated it. It was the bear, however, that was the real danger, at least when it felt that its young were threatened. The wolf and the leopard were also among the shepherd's traditional enemies. David does not mention them, but he must have encountered them at one time or another.

and learnt how to use a sling against them. He had also learnt how to benefit from the long days of overwhelming heat when the flock took shelter together under a terebinth and he practised on the zither.[3] Among the Hebrews, as generally throughout the East, the player was also a singer, and his instrument was principally used for the accompaniment. In addition, he was usually a poet, and the music formed a background to his poetical improvisations.

David was an extremely attractive young man, of pleasing appearance, and gifted as a poet and musician. These qualities were to prove useful to him.

David, the young shepherd, is anointed

Samuel was still living in Ramah, bemoaning the ills that must soon fall upon Saul and, through him, upon the people also. Then, one day on instructions from Yahweh, he filled a ram's horn with oil and set out for Bethlehem. Saul kept a constant watch on his movements and Samuel, to avoid arousing suspicion, took with him a heifer, saying publicly that he was going to offer a sacrifice to Yahweh. On arriving at Bethlehem he at once approached its elders, who made no secret of their anxiety at having to receive the king's opponent. From among the elders present he picked out Jesse and invited him and his seven sons to take part in the sacred meal. Each of the young men was introduced to him in turn. He scrutinized them carefully and tried to penetrate their characters. But although

[3] Specialists in early instruments now agree that David, at first as a shepherd and then at Saul's court, played on the kinnor (1 Sam. 16: 16). David's instrument may well have been the zither that appears in the famous fresco of Beni-Hassan, in which Asiatics are shown playing this species of harp. Briefly described, it had a sounding-board of about twenty inches by twelve, and hollow at the top. It had eight parallel strings, stretched horizontally, and plucked by the left hand, these provided the melody of the song. Three or four strings were stretched across the sounding board, and manipulated by the right hand which, with the aid of a plectrum of dark wood, played the accompaniment.

he appreciated their physical and moral qualities he realized that it was not upon any of these that God's choice had fallen. He asked Jesse whether he had no other sons, and received the answer that there was in fact one more[4] who at the moment was looking after the sheep. Samuel fastened on this last hope and requested that he should be found immediately. He decided that they would not form the usual circle, (that is, sitting on the ground with the dish in the centre), until the young man arrived.

David came at last, and as soon as he saw him, Samuel was convinced that this was God's chosen one. He took the horn of oil and poured its contents upon the young man's head. After this anointing[5] *the spirit of Yahweh seized on David and stayed with him from that day on* (1 Sam. 16: 13). Without further delay, Samuel went back to his home in Ramah.

The shepherd David makes a dramatic entry into Saul's capital

Two different traditions exist about David's early years, but they coincide on the issue of Goliath. They record the circumstances which enabled the Judaean shepherd to enter the king of Israel's court. The first tradition describes David as a singer and harpist who

[4] It seems, however, that David really had only three brothers (1 Sam. 17: 13–15). The eight brethren of 1 Sam. 16: 10 is very probably an embellishment of the narrative.

[5] We have already seen that Samuel had personally anointed Saul while the latter was in search of his father's donkeys. The anointing of David in Bethlehem, on the other hand, had an essentially family setting. It seems that these were *private* anointings which should be distinguished from those *royal* anointings, carried out by a priest or a prophet in the presence of the assembled people, as a solemn hallowing of the man chosen by Yahweh. The two anointings, so far mentioned, of Saul and David, (without witnesses in the case of Saul: and within a narrow family circle in that of David) should be taken as symbolic, a sign of God's choice. It was a hidden liturgical action that may well have long remained without any outward manifestation – as indeed happened in the two instances mentioned.

And whenever the spirit from God troubled Saul, David took the harp and played; then Saul grew calm, and recovered, and the evil spirit left him.

1 Sam. 16 : 23

finally went with Saul into battle. The second describes the conflict between David the young shepherd and Goliath, a Philistine giant. Both narratives are here first summarized and then subjected to a critical examination.

Saul had been deeply affected by Samuel's curse, and experienced the assault of an *evil spirit* which caused him deep melancholy. He was then told of a shepherd from Judah, who had some repute as a poet and musician; he played the zither, sang and composed poetry in praise of God. He was a man of presence and Yahweh was with him. His talents would take the king's mind off his sickness, and perhaps disperse the gloomy ideas that beset him. A messenger was at once dispatched to Jesse, asking for his son to be sent to the court at Gibeah. Jesse quickly obeyed the royal command, and sent the young musician to the king together with a gift of five loaves, a skin of wine and a kid, (1 Sam. 16: 20) – an indication of the primitive nature of the civilization.

With his natural grace and that charm that never left him throughout his long life, David managed to introduce a note of cheerfulness and liveliness into that gloomy little court. As soon as the unhappy king was attacked by a fit of melancholy, David took his zither, gently struck its strings and sang sweetly. The crisis ended immediately. Very soon Saul could not do without him, and required him to be constantly at his side. He thus became one of the court favourites. He even became the king's armour-bearer, and as such had the honour of carrying the royal shield in battle, and of being at the king's side in hand-to-hand fighting. Saul then sent to Jesse saying: *'Let David enter my service; he has won my favour.'* In this way, therefore, the young shepherd from Bethlehem began to make his way towards becoming one of the important figures of Saul's court.

But there is another version of how David came to be associated with Saul; it is that which describes the fight between the young shepherd and the Philistine giant (1 Sam. 17).

The Philistines had been driven back from central Canaan. They were now trying to infiltrate further south into the heights of Judah. From their bases at Gath and Ekron, they advanced by way of Azekah, as far as Bethlehem, sixteen miles south-west of Jerusalem. It was a clever move, because if the Philistines were victorious they would gain control of the valleys running up to Bethlehem and Hebron, and, in practice, of the whole southern region.

In spite of his neurotic attacks, Saul was still a great captain. He decided to make a stand against the enemy's attack on the tribes of Simeon and Judah in the south. With a body of picked troops he moved to the key point and set up his camp close to Socoh in the Valley of the Terebinth, on the slope facing the enemy forces. A deep wadi separated the two armies.

Why did both armies pause before coming to grips? This was in accordance with an ancient custom; before the encounter each side showered insults on the other. The practice originated in religious magic; it was a way of invoking the wrath of the gods upon the enemy.

In this case, however, the delay had a different and more realistic explanation. Goliath, a Philistine champion, came out every morning and, hurling abuse and insult, tried to provoke the Israelites. Let one of them, he said, make up his mind to engage him in a personal encounter. In this way the issue between the two sides could be settled.

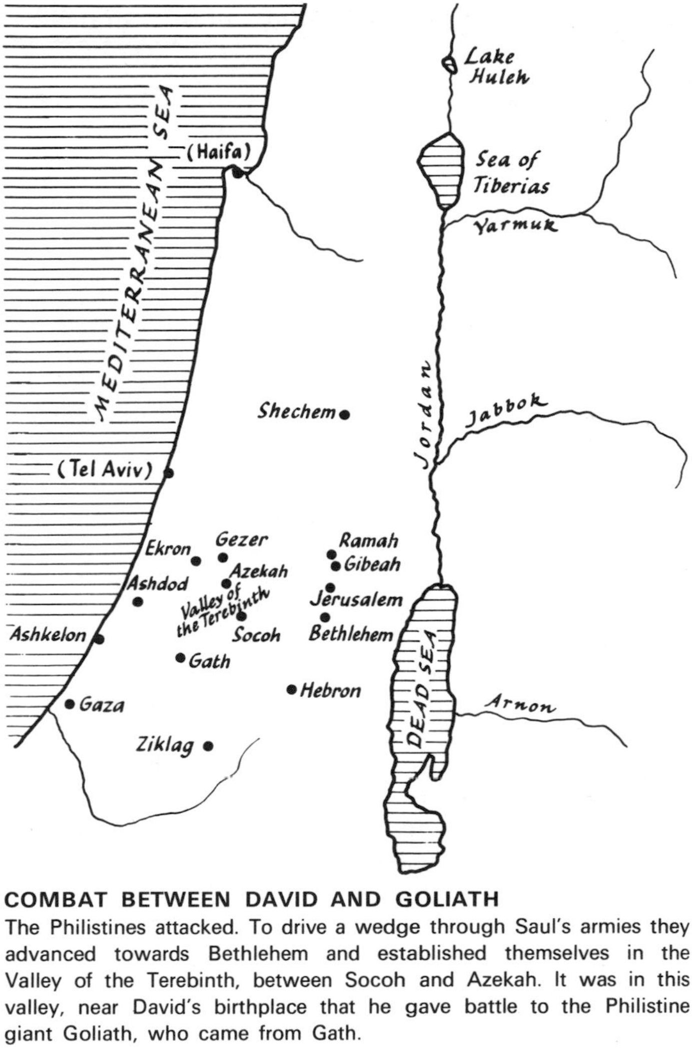

COMBAT BETWEEN DAVID AND GOLIATH

The Philistines attacked. To drive a wedge through Saul's armies they advanced towards Bethlehem and established themselves in the Valley of the Terebinth, between Socoh and Azekah. It was in this valley, near David's birthplace that he gave battle to the Philistine giant Goliath, who came from Gath.

After the death of Goliath the Israelite armies pursued the Philistines to the gates of Gath and Ekron.

This Philistine, a native of Gath, was of enormous stature; he was six cubits and one span (that is, just over nine and a half feet) tall. Even allowing for some exaggeration on the part of the narrator, he must have been a giant of exceptional proportions. His equipment was equally formidable: a bronze helmet; a breastplate of scale-armour; bronze greaves on his legs – a typical feature of Aegean civilization. He brandished a huge spear with a lancing socket – a detail also found in Greek and Egyptian bas-reliefs. In his belt he wore a bronze sword. A shield-bearer walked in front of him to ward off the enemy's arrows and javelins.

Among the Hebrews it was only a few of the senior officers who were equipped with a sword or lance, and in any case their weapons were light. The troops had bows and some spears; they also had slings that enabled them to fight at a distance – a prudent precaution; these slings were handled with great skill by men of experience.

Three of David's brothers were in the ranks. Jesse, who was still living in Bethlehem, decided to send some food to his sons serving in the forces. Accordingly, he sent David, the youngest, to his elder brothers, with an ephah of roasted grain and ten loaves. He also added ten cheeses for their commanding officer, (the head of a 'thousand'). He told David to ask after his brothers' health, and to bring back some *token* as a guarantee that the gift had been well received.

David reached the camp and leaving the bundle in charge of the baggage guard, ran to the battle line and went to ask his brothers how they were. They gave him a somewhat cool reception. "*Why have you come down here?*' they asked, 'Whom have you left in charge of the sheep? Is it to watch the battle that you are come here?'

Just at this moment, Goliath again put in an appearance. As usual he issued his round of curses and jeeringly repeated his challenge. David asked for an explanation. Some soldiers described the position, and added that the king would lavish riches upon the man who should kill the Philistine, besides giving him his daughter in marriage and exemption from taxes and forced labour. David immediately made up his mind: he would fight the Philistine.

There was general astonishment at this announcement. The unknown youth explained that at home, on the plain, he looked after his father's sheep and was used to combating wild beasts. Therefore he would be able to deal with this man who had *dared to insult the armies of the living God*. Saul, convinced at last, replied: *'Go, and Yahweh be with you'*. But before the encounter, it was decided to equip the slender champion with the king's own armour. But with Saul's heavy breastplate over his shoulders – it must be remembered that Saul was a huge man – David found that he was unable to walk. So he decided to approach the enemy with his staff alone. In his shepherd's bag he put five smooth stones from the river, and concealed his sling by folding it in his hand. This piece of cunning on his part ensured that he would not be taken for a combatant slinger; he had not put the stones in a soldier's wallet, but in a shepherd's satchel, and he was careful not to show his sling. At the sight of him, Goliath would think that it was a shepherd from the Judean hills who confronted him.

The Philistine giant saw this slight young man coming towards him. He was amazed. On either side of the valley, separated by the stream, the opposing armies watched this strange sight.

Foolishly, Goliath lost his temper: *'Am I a dog for*

you to come against me with sticks?' he shouted, and added, contemptuously: *'Come over here and I will give your flesh to the birds of the air and the beasts of the field.'* David's reply was instant and vivid: *'You come against me with sword and spear and javelin, but I come against you in the name of Yahweh Sabaoth, the God of the armies of Israel that you have dared to insult. Today Yahweh will deliver you into my hand, and I shall kill you; I will cut off your head . . . so that all the earth may know that there is a God in Israel, and that all this assembly may know that it is not by sword or by spear that Yahweh gives the victory, for Yahweh is lord of the battle and he will deliver you into our power.'*

Matters thereupon hurried to a close. Goliath, strongly protected by his breastplate, had not bothered to take his armour-bearer as a guard; his opponent was too contemptible. He approached with his lance raised. David quickly took a stone from his satchel, and put it in the sling he had learnt to use so well against the wild beasts of the plain. He whirled the sling and before the giant could even realize that his puny opponent was attacking him, he received a violent blow in mid-forehead. He fell to the ground, unconscious. David rushed forward and taking hold of the Philistine's great sword cut off his head before he had time to come to his senses.

From the ranks of Israel shouts of triumph burst forth; from those of the Philistines, cries of terror; Yahweh himself was fighting with the Hebrews. Saul led his forces, now wildly elated, and drove the enemy back to the walls of its fortresses of Gath and Ekron.

David picked up the head of Goliath; his cloak and sword were collected and put behind the ephod in the sanctuary of Nob, as an act of homage to Yahweh for giving strength to him who had no sword or spear.

According to this account, Saul did not as yet know David. After the latter's victory, the king grew curious about his family and background.[6] Having received information on these points, Saul decided to keep near him the young warrior who had given such an example of incomparable courage to the most tried soldiers of Israel. Jonathan, Saul's eldest son and the heir to the throne, took the opportunity of expressing his soldierly admiration for David, and formed on the spot a pact of friendship with the victor which was never thereafter broken; following the ancient Semitic tradition, the two young men sealed this pact by exchanging cloaks, belts and weapons.

The question now arises as to whether David first came to be a member of Saul's court as a harpist, or, as in this narrative, because of the impression he made upon the king through his great achievement in overthrowing Goliath. Formerly, many scholars tried to explain the two accounts by making them agree fundamentally. But today most critics incline to the view that the two traditions must have existed separately for a very long time before a scribe combined them together. But, in the present state of our knowledge, no real solution of this small historical problem can be offered. Both traditions agree on two points only: David was a young shepherd from Bethlehem who, in an unexpected way, became a member of the king's court.

David becomes a popular hero

Whatever the means, there can be no doubt that David quickly secured an important position in the somewhat primitive court of Gibeah, and that this

[6] In the East, a stranger is not asked: who are you; but, who is your father.

position became steadily stronger. To begin with, he won the king's favour; Saul seemed to have appreciated very fully the artistic and military qualities of his armour-bearer, and periodically he entrusted him with picked troops to carry out brief expeditions against the Philistines. Then he was Jonathan's admiring friend. And, lastly, through his own military exploits, he showed that he was a superlative tactician, even though, after an encounter, he modestly disclaimed any credit.

When he came back from these expeditions against the Philistines, and passed through the villages of Israel, the women came out singing and dancing in their joy to the accompaniment of tambourines; their refrain has come down to us:

'Saul has killed his thousands,
And David his tens of thousands.'

In this way, Jesse's son, the hitherto unknown little shepherd, acquired the dimensions of a hero. No ambition seemed beyond him, and a wonderful future appeared to beckon him.

Saul's rages against David (1 Sam. 18: 6–16)
Saul was constantly haunted by the fear that a rival would drive him from power. Samuel's prophecy made him fear the worst, and very soon David's social and military success gave fresh impetus to his gloomy thoughts. He observed bitterly: *'They have given David his tens of thousands, but me only the thousands; he has all but the kingship now.'* Jealousy quickly developed in his disordered brain, and his affection for David turned to fear and hatred.

On two occasions, when David was playing on his

On the following day an evil spirit from God seized on Saul and he fell into a fit of frenzy while he was in his house. David was playing the harp as on other days and Saul had his spear in his hand. Saul brandished the spear; 'I am going to pin David to the wall' he said. But David twice evaded him.

1 Sam. 18:10–11

harp in an attempt to soothe the king's melancholy, Saul took his spear – the symbol of royal authority that had to be always within reach – and threw it suddenly, intending to pin David to the wall. But David was on his guard and managed to evade it.

On the whole, it seemed wiser to get rid of this rival by sending him on military expeditions of especial danger. But from each of these he came back not only safe and sound, but with increased reputation.

Saul had thought of giving him his eldest daughter Merab in marriage, but going back on his word, gave her instead to a man named Adriel. However, Saul's second daughter, Michal, fell in love with David and Saul decided to give her to him. But David was hesitant and said to the king's servants: *'Does it strike you as an easy thing for me to become the king's son-in-law, poor and of humble position as I am?'* He was referring to the *mohar*, the sum which had to be paid by the bridegroom to his future father-in-law, as the purchase price for his wife. He was obviously unable to raise the large amount required for a king's daughter, and he said so. He was told that he was mistaken. Saul did not want any money but only a hundred foreskins of the Philistines. This would prove that the enemies he killed were really 'uncircumcised'. Of course, Saul hoped that he would be killed on this dangerous expedition. A hundred victims was a considerable number and implied a whole series of hazardous encounters. But Saul's secret purpose was not achieved. David returned victorious, bringing *two hundred* of these trophies, twice the number originally demanded. *He counted them out before the king, so that he could become the king's son-in-law*. And, in fact, Michal became his wife.

Saul's morbid attacks became increasingly frequent.

Sometimes his attitude to David seemed to be one of genuine fatherly affection. But very often David's very existence hung on a thread.

David in a position of great danger

In the circle of his advisers and friends Saul could only see traitors and spies, and David became the object of his especial hate. The Philistines had failed to kill this undesirable person; Saul felt that he had better see to it himself. The murder was decided on, and the details of the plot were secretly decided upon.

One day Michal noticed that the house was surrounded. It would not be long before the king's agents entered. She immediately warned her husband: *'If you do not escape tonight, you will be a dead man tomorrow.'*

In parenthesis: David and the Psalms

The narrative must here be briefly interrupted in order to observe David in a new light, that of 'the psalmist'.

There is a dramatic fitness in discussing the matter at this point. Saul's agents were about to enter the house. David's life seemed to be nearing its end. He took his harp and addressed a fervent prayer to Yahweh, begging him, in his mercy, to save him from this imminent danger. This was expressed in the lyrical notes of Psalm 59,[7] accompanied on the harp in the traditional way. Some scholars ascribe this great poem to the events related here. The appeal to the Almighty begins with this heart-rending cry:

[7] *Of David. When Saul sent spies to his house to have him killed.* These titles and inscriptions of the Psalms must be taken simply as indications, inserted later. They are often questionable.

Rescue me from my enemies, my God
protect me from those attacking me,
rescue me from these evil men,
save me from these murderers.

As the events of David's life unfold, the poems that David may have composed in relation to them will be referred to in this context. But the question at once arises: should David be considered to be the author of the Psalms? And if not, can any of them be attributed to him with some degree of certainty? At this point we must insert a brief but necessary parenthesis, for in these volumes the historical criticism of the Psalms as a whole will not be discussed again.

The word 'psalm' is directly derived from the Greek *psalterion*, a stringed instrument used for accompanying the singing of a poem. The musical directions at the beginning of each Psalm mean little to us. They frequently indicate a tune, known to the people, (to the tune: 'Of the lilies'; to that of 'The Doe of the Dawn'; 'For sickness', etc) according to which a given psalm should be sung.

The psalter in the Bible contains 150 psalms. Formerly, an excessive traditionalism insisted that it was entirely David's creation. At the end of the last century, the ultra-critical school fell into the opposite extreme; these historians held that not a single psalm had David as its author. Today, a wide range of biblical scholars adopt a less rigid attitude, and divide the psalms into three main categories:—

1. Those earlier than David, of which some fragments have come down to us.

2. Those later than David, the work of various inspired scribes during the period of the kings, or in the centuries after the return from the Babylonian Exile (538 B.C.).

3. Those composed at the time of David, whose authors were:

(a) Professional cantors (the sons of Korah; the sons of Asaph, etc); their work was to write the liturgical music to be performed before the Ark in the Temple of Yahweh in Jerusalem.

(b) David himself. In the course of this work will be mentioned in chronological order, those psalms which, partly or in their entirety, may be attributed to him.

About half of the Psalter may be by David – unless some of the psalms ascribed to him, are in fact simply 'dedicated' to him. Sound criticism is forced to admit that a number of them bear the marks of his genius. But each example must be discussed on its own merits. The difficulties encountered by literary criticism and philological investigation are due to the fact that in the course of centuries, the various psalms attributed to David underwent revision and correction, and received fresh additions. They were in constant use in worship in the Temple and, later, in synagogues. In the course of the centuries of use they would very probably have been modified and expanded.

David escapes from the fortress of Gibeah

Michal said to her husband: *'If you do not escape tonight, you will be a dead man tomorrow.'* Taking advantage of the dusk, he escaped through a window.

It was just in time. Saul's agents soon arrived to lay hold of his son-in-law. To gain time, and to enable her husband to get ahead of his pursuers, Michal arranged a clever deception. She put a *teraphim*[8]

[8] Teraphim. This obviously had nothing in common with the little idols which Rachel stole from her father and hid in the pack-saddle of her camel (cf Isaac and Jacob, p. 66) Michal's teraphim however must have been life-size. It is surprising that an idol of this kind should have had a place in authentic Yahwist circles, for this cult belonged to early Semitic beliefs. Was the teraphim described here Michal's personal property? Did David merely tolerate it in his

in her husband's bed, covered it with a garment and put a truss of goat's hair on its head. When her father's men arrived, she pointed to the dummy, and said: '*He is ill*,' and dismissed them without more ado. Discomforted, they made their report to Saul who at once fell into a great rage. He told them to go back to David's home and seize him. '*Bring him to me on his bed*,' he shouted, '*for me to kill him*.' But it was far too late. David had already escaped.

He stopped en route at Ramah, where he paid a visit to Samuel. The old prophet seemed uncertain what he could do about the king of Israel of whose conduct, however, he still disapproved. But he prayed that Yahweh would protect the young man from Bethlehem whom he had anointed with the holy oil.

Jonathan, David's great friend, did his utmost to effect a reconciliation. He began by cautiously sounding his father but Saul replied with insults and with threats of death for David. He cursed his son, and in a dramatic interview, tried to kill him. There was not the least hope of settling matters, the king's mind was driven towards crime. With great difficulty, Jonathan managed to meet David in the fields. He gave him an impartial account of the position. They shed many tears together, and when they parted, Jonathan spoke the traditional words: '*Go in peace*.' They said good-bye with heavy hearts, and David took the road to the south, the road to exile.

David joins the resistance

After his great period as a victor, David now entered

house? Or did he also have recourse to this instrument of divination? It must be added at once that the way in which it was questioned, or the methods used in interpreting its supposed replies, are not known. For the historian, it all remains shrouded in obscurity. The scribe's prejudiced account should be noted; he was opposed to this practice with its magical aspect, and stressed the somewhat comic function of the idol used for this trick.

his time of trial. The former leader of Israel's armies had become an outlaw. And time, far from easing the position, made it worse. It was not a promising development, and it had four results.

First of all, David appears as a mere fugitive, compelled by prudence to run away. But Saul soon set out in furious pursuit of his former subordinate; and then matters developed into serious guerilla warfare.

This, however, in no way prevented David from carrying out a shrewd policy of matrimonial alliances in the south; he seems cleverly to have prepared for the future.

But ultimately the conflict between Saul's army and that of the former shepherd of Bethlehem and his group of outlaws, proved radically unequal. So David gave it up, and went over to the hereditary enemy, the Philistines. Did this mean that his adventure was over?

David, the outlaw in flight (See map, p. 87)

Ancient traditions record several vivid and colourful incidents in the fugitive's wandering life.

His first stop was at Nob, a short distance from Gibeah, identified today as Mount Scopus, east of Jerusalem. Ahimelech, the priest of the place, was a descendant of Eli; the Shiloh priests had fled to Nob after the city, in which the Ark was kept, had been destroyed. Ahimelech expressed some surprise at seeing the king's son-in-law without arms or escort. David, never at a loss for an explanation, said that he had been obliged to leave Gibeah in haste and had agreed to meet his men a little further on. In the hurry of his departure, he had had no time to take a sword, and he asked Ahimelech to give him Goliath's; this memorable trophy had been reverently placed *behind the ephod*[9] of the temple.

He also asked Ahimelech to give him food, but the priest had only consecrated loaves to offer him – little rolls put 'before Yahweh' in the sanctuary, and, in principle, reserved to the priests. Ahimelech hesitated for a moment, but then considered that a relative of the king could not be allowed to starve. He asked David whether he was in a state of ritual purity (that is abstaining from sexual intercourse). David answered that soldiers on active service always were. And then, with Goliath's sword and the sacred loaves, he resumed his journey.

He decided to make his way to the territory of the Philistines. There he would be safe from Saul's enquiries. He approached Gath, Goliath's native city. But as soon as he arrived he was recognised and pursued. As a measure of security he played the madman. The gates were then opened to him, for in ancient times, insanity was thought to give its victim a sacred and inviolable character.[10]

After reflection, in the circumstances he decided that

[9] Another instrument used in divination. It will be discussed again shortly. David used it throughout his period of exile as a means of questioning Yahweh. It is clear that Canaanite ritual magic had penetrated deeply into Yahwist circles.

[10] Psalm 56 may have been composed at this time. Some believe that it contains ancient elements and that David may well have been its author. It begins with an appeal to the Almighty:

Take pity on me, God, as they harry me, . . .
All day my opponents harry me.

It ends in thanksgiving:

for you have rescued me from Death
to walk in the presence of God
in the light of the living

As regards Psalm 34, the inscription at the beginning asserting it to have been composed by David in thanksgiving to God for enabling him to leave Gath, is open to serious question. At least in its present acrostic form – each verse beginning with a different letter, in the order of the Hebrew alphabet – it is certainly of a date later than the Babylonian Exile, the return from which occurred in 538 B.C.

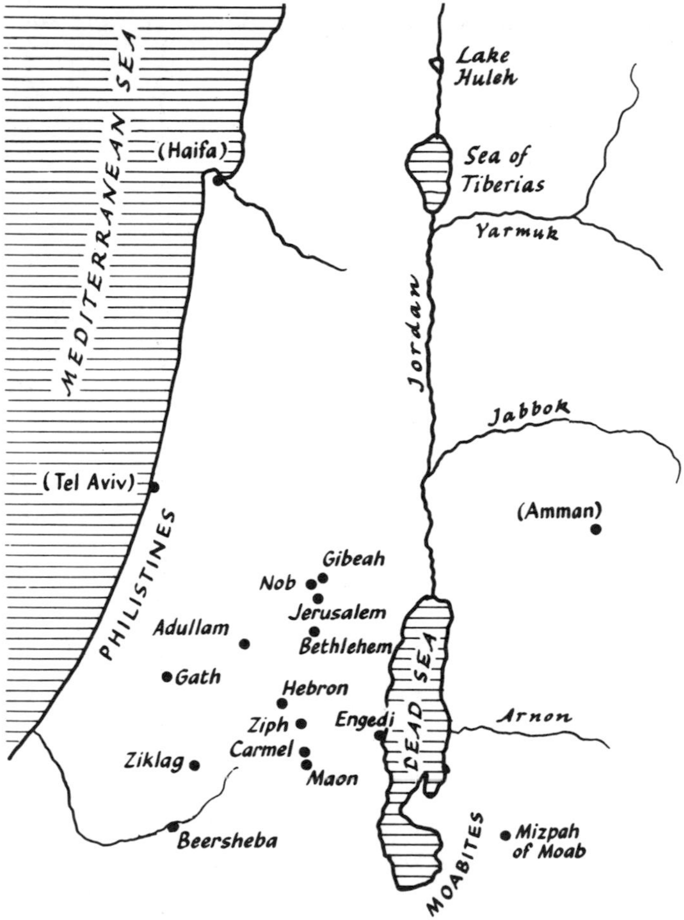

DAVID'S FLIGHT FROM SAUL

To escape a worse plight David was obliged to flee from the royal court at Gibeah where Saul reigned. He went by way of Nob, and sought refuge at Gath in Philistia. Then he returned to Judah. He thought it advisable to take his family to Moab (south-east of the Dead Sea) where he placed his family in safety.

Adventures in the cave of Engedi; then in the desert of Ziph. In the end to escape Saul's vengeance David was obliged to leave his own country. Once more he went to Philistia and gave his services to Achish, king of Gath, who admitted him as a vassal and gave him the territories of Ziklag.

his most prudent course was to return to Judah. So he took refuge in the Cave of Adullam, a kind of natural citadel, west of Bethlehem. It is a hilly and comparatively well-watered neighbourhood. He was now no longer alone; he had been joined by relatives and friends against whom the law of the blood-feud automatically came into force.

He immediately became the leader of the resistance, a respected head of four hundred outlaws – homeless men, rebels, malcontents and adventurers. They managed to exist by means of raids, marauding, robbery and violence.

He was anxious to preserve freedom of movement and therefore decided to keep his family away from the conflicts in which he was inevitably involved. He took them to Moab, on the east of the Dead Sea, then he came back to the hills of Judah and awaited events. The king's forces were unquestionably superior, but he had by no means lost hope. He realized that at any moment he might have to meet Saul's men, but even with his mere handful of supporters he was ready to oppose them.

Saul's strange way of opening hostilities

Saul's reply to David's action against him was the slaughter of the priestly body at Nob. Had not its priest Ahimelech given the sacred loaves to David as food? Had he not surrendered Goliath's sword? Ahimelech received this accusation at Gibeah, and defended himself adroitly: David had come to Nob, as he had often done before, when he needed to consult the oracle. It was true that during his last visit he had been received with honour, and that he had given him the little he possessed, and since David was ritually clean no religious crime could be attributed to him. As for Goliath's sword, it was the commander of the royal armies who had asked for it; it was his by right, since his particular duty was to fight for Israel. Ahimelech had had no information about the dispute between the king and David (a questionable assertion) and had acted in complete loyalty.

Saul was unmoved: the priest deserved death; and accordingly, he, and his whole family were slaughtered.[11] The Edomite Doeg alone agreed to perform the massacre. Only one of Ahimelech's sons, Abiathar, managed to escape to David with the ephod he had taken, unobserved, from the sanctuary. David received it with great feeling. He now possessed the instrument of divination which had hitherto been used by the ministers at Shiloh, and he also had at hand the priest who could ask the questions and interpret the answer. According to contemporary ideas, this meant that Yahweh would give this little band the benefit of his counsel and lead it to victory.

Saul's one idea: David's capture

It was the usual story of conflict between a well-equipped and organized army and a small band of guerillas, constantly retreating and yet always ready to surprise the enemy at the least expected moment.

Saul's attitude was the result of a fixed idea in a sick and unbalanced mind. David, a leader of first-rate ability might well have provided Saul with priceless assistance in his conflicts with the Philistines. Saul made every effort to track him down, and his failure

[11] At that time David had taken refuge in the desert of Negeb, and he was saddened to learn of the murder of the priest of Nob who had fed him. The inscription of Psalm 52 suggests that when he received this news, he composed these verses against Doeg the traitor, who had been one of the agents in this sad business. Modern scholars, however, consider that it really belongs to the time of Jeremiah (645 – 587).

aggravated his jealousy, his anger and his fits of depression.

By this time, David's men had increased to six hundred; they were rough fellows, perhaps not very dependable, but well experienced in fighting. The way they repulsed a Philistine raid at Keilah affords a preliminary notion of their bravery and of their leader's skill.

Saul, unhappily, was never able to view the situation objectively. For David only wanted to be restored to favour, to regain his place at court and his position as leader of the king's forces. But Saul sank even deeper into the abyss of his murderous ideas. He foresaw that one day Yahweh would place this young man on the throne. He became obsessed with a single idea: how to get rid of his rival. This made him even neglect the danger from the Philistines.

David confronts Saul (See map, p. 87)

It was a desperate cat and mouse pursuit, but the mouse was never caught. Both the writer and the reader inevitably sympathize with the young and always quick-witted hero. David was frequently near capture, but he always slipped through his enemy's hands.

Only two characteristic episodes illustrating the mentality of the times need be mentioned here: the first occurred at the cave at Engedi, the second at Ziph.

The district of Engedi, on the banks of the Dead Sea, is a stony wilderness. David had narrowly escaped one of Saul's patrols and taken refuge in a deep and gloomy cave.[12] Into this cave came Saul, in order to *cover his*

[12] David is on the point of being captured. Psalm 142: Prayer of a hunted man:

To Yahweh, my cry! I plead.
To Yahweh, my cry! I entreat.
I pour out my supplications . . .

feet (a traditional biblical expression for 'to relieve himself'). David crept up to him unobserved, and cut off the border of his cloak. His men were about to lay hold of Saul, but David restrained them, saying: *'He is the anointed of Yahweh.'*

Without being aware of the deadly danger he had just escaped, Saul left the cave. David followed him and called out: *'My lord king!'* Saul looked round; David bowed to the ground and did homage, and then, keeping his distance, showed him the border of his cloak and explained that he could have killed him easily, but had not done so. He begged Saul to realize that *'there is neither malice nor treason in my mind. I have not offended against you, yet you hunt me down to take my life. May Yahweh be judge between me and you . . . May Yahweh be the judge . . . take up my cause and free me from your power'* (1 Sam. 24).

Saul wept. *'You are a more upright man than I'*, he said and concluded by prophesying that David would indeed reign and that the sovereignty of Israel would be secure in his hands.[13] He asked David to spare his descendants, should they ever fall into his hands. Then they parted, and David and his men went back to the stronghold. About this time, Samuel died in Ramah.

Saul still kept on the track of his elusive enemy, and we meet them both again in the desert of Ziph.[14]

[13] Psalm 57: David's thanksgiving to God:

I mean to sing and play for you,
awake my muse,
awake, lyre and harp,
I mean to wake the dawn.

[14] The town of Ziph, built on the hill now known as Tel el-Zif, about two miles south-east of Hebron. The wilderness of Ziph, one of the divisions of the arid wilderness of Judah, lay between the hill and the Dead Sea.

The Ziphites, who supported Saul, kept him informed about David's movements. Hence Psalm 54:

God save me by your name
by your power see justice done to me.

It is an ancient composition, and may be by David.

Saul had established himself on the Hill of Hachilah on top of the plain. By evening he had set up his tents, and surrounded by soldiers, retired to rest. Together with his friend Abishai, David inspected the approaches to the camp and saw that it would be possible to slide through the circle of sentinels. With a little skill, they managed to get behind the enclosure formed by the ring of defences, and at nightfall reached the tent in which Saul was sleeping. Abishai wanted to pin him to the ground with his own spear, but David restrained him; all he wanted was to take Saul's spear, fixed in the ground by his side, and the pitcher of water to quench his thirst during the night. They took these things and then leaving the camp, climbed the slope overlooking the tents, and shouted to Saul to show the objects they had just taken from him. The royal army, awakened by this noise, was soon alert. The king came out of his tent. When he saw that his spear and pitcher were in David's hands, he realized the magnanimity of the man whom he pursued with hatred. Although Saul begged David to come back, his prudence restrained him. But the whole incident may be just another version of the encounter at Engedi.

David, the leader of rebellion

For David, the position was now clear. It was a waste of time to hope any longer that the king's court might be won over. He was now firmly established on the heights of Judah. Against his own will, he had become the leader of an armed band of rebels in the full sense of the word.

The adventurers he had gathered around him were always on a war footing. During this disturbed period, the farm-workers in every district needed the protection of these soldiers against the ravages of robbers, always ready for raids and plunder. Sometimes, indeed, this improvised army imposed its own services and fixed its own reward – it was, in fact, a rudimentary feudal organization. But this did not mean that these alien custodians who secured peace in one area, might not produce chaos in another by their plundering activities.

We noticed earlier that David exercised a peculiar fascination over his comrades. His personal attractiveness, allied to a mature sense of justice most uncommon at this period, together with his unconquerable energy qualified by very human sensitivity made him a leader reverenced throughout the kingdom. His original allies were constantly being reinforced by fresh forces of a very different calibre. Veterans, famous for their exploits, were eager to submit to his command. Officers who had served under Saul were happy to serve under this leader whose qualities they had previously discerned.

On one occasion eleven Gadites (Hebrews from Transjordania), men of legendary courage, crossed the Jordan and came to join David's little army. After them came recruits from Judah.

We can follow him in his wanderings through Carmel in Judah (not to be confused with Carmel in Jezreel), Ziph, Horesh and Maon; he became the self-styled protector of the farmers of the region who, willingly or unwillingly, had to guarantee that his men were fed.

In his native Judah, too, he pursued his carefully calculated policy. Saul used his son-in-law's departure as a pretext for taking back Michal and re-marrying her to a Benjaminite, Palti, the son of Laish. He intended that this should eliminate David from the throne, and also insult him publicly. David, thus repudiated by his father-in-law, made two fresh marriages in the south: the first was with Ahinoam, a woman of the clan of Caleb; she bore him Amnon, his eldest son: the second was also with a Calebite, Abigail, the widow of Nabal, a wealthy landowner of the neighbourhood.

David takes refuge with the Philistines

In the end, in order to get beyond the reach of Saul's wrath, David, guarded by his soldiers, reluctantly found it necessary to leave the land which was sacred to Yahweh. Accordingly, he sought refuge with Achish, the king of Gath, one of the five Philistine sovereigns. He offered him his services, and, now and then, helped him with his men. This was an astonishing reversal of positions for a man who had formerly fought the Philistines with such vigour. Achish welcomed him warmly, and gave him the town and territory of Ziklag on the frontier between Philistia and Judah, north-east of Beersheba.

The Philistine princeling may well have been delighted to see David anxious to strike a blow against Israel. He probably thought that Saul's ex-son-in-law could be counted on to give free rein to his feelings of revenge and to lay waste his lands. But David was too keen a politician to be caught in this way. He was determined to maintain good relations with his religious brethren, who might in time become his subjects. On returning from an expedition he went to his Philistine overlord to give him his share of the booty. Achish asked him the name of the tribe against which he had carried out his raid. But David had seen what was in his mind, and said that he had been attacking a body of Judaeans, Jerahmeelites or Kenites. Achish pretended to believe him, but everyone knew that in fact he had aimed his blow against the southern Amalekites, Israel's constant enemies.

Through this astute and far-seeing policy, David quickly secured the sympathy of the Hebrew leaders, who realised that he deliberately avoided bringing destruction and misery into the cities or countryside of Israel. In view of this, more and more of the southern Israelites came to join the outlaw. Indeed, people had had more than enough of the half-crazed Saul.

About this time David saw a score of Benjaminites approaching. They were Saul's relatives and warriors, and they wanted to enter the exile's service.

David's life as a rebel leader in Philistia, following his guerilla warfare in Israel, had fashioned his character. He became recognised as a supremely talented soldier. Evidently he was also a cunning diplomat, able to come to terms with the hereditary enemy, the Philistines, and yet maintain the admiring sympathy of the Israelites. And he continued to develop those moral qualities of wisdom and justice which would be so important when he finally became king.

For the moment, however, he was still an insignificant partisan, doubtless a resistance leader of genius, but so far, insignificant compared either with the head of the Israelite league or with the rulers of the Philistine confederation. It looked as though the former shepherd from Bethlehem had reached the highest position of which he was capable. It appeared that he would pass the rest of his life in exile, serving the Philistine princelings.

He had been in Philistine territory for about a year. His life had been mediocre, that of a refugee, a mercenary, a vassal, a leader of a rebel band without much future. But events soon radically altered his position.

Philistine ambitions (See map, p. 98)

The Philistines were restricted to central Canaan, and for some time did not dare to renew their attacks against Saul's forces. A policy of infiltration seemed more prudent, especially in the south where their hands were freer. But becoming bolder again, they decided to make a very special effort and try to seize the whole of the plain of Jezreel.

David's ambiguous position

The rulers of the five Philistine cities concentrated their forces on Aphek, on the coastal plain at the foot of Mount Ephraim. As Achish's vassal, David was strictly obliged to march with the Philistine armies against 'the enemy' – in this case, against Israel, the men of his own blood and servants of Yahweh. Achish had even promised to make David his 'bodyguard' on the battle-field – a tragic position for a man of integrity and a worshipper of God.

Fortunately, however, circumstances worked in David's favour. When the Philistines met at Aphek and prepared their plan of attack, some of their leaders declared that it would be extremely foolish to put a Hebrew in such a position of trust. Would not David be tempted – especially if, in the beginning, fortune smiled on Israel – to fall away, join Saul's forces and turn against his Philistine masters? In previous engagements, Hebrew mercenaries, thoughtlessly recruited by the Philistines, had been observed to change sides in this way. The Philistine commanders, therefore, decided that David must go back to the district assigned to him at Ziklag. He was not needed for the battle. Achish was extremely embarrassed, but he tried to explain to David that he would not be allowed to join the Philistine army.

David was never lacking in diplomatic finesse. He at once protested that his intentions were honest and pretended to be very hurt by this lack of respect. Inwardly, he was probably most pleased by this providential solution that had saved him from a very difficult situation. If he had spilt Hebrew blood, the magnificent future he had begun to foresee would have been irremediably compromised.

He went back to Ziklag in Philistine territory, where, with his men, he meant to await quietly the result of the battle. Unfortunately, however, when he arrived, he found the place in ruins. It had been laid waste and burnt by Amalekite plunderers, taking advantage of David's temporary absence. All its inhabitants – men, women and children – had been taken away by the relentless raiders to the Negeb wilderness. Their destiny was obvious. They would be sold to the Egyptian slave merchants, for the Amalekites were their accredited suppliers. The flocks would be a most attractive proposition to these highway robbers.

Abiathar the priest, the sole survivor from the massacre at Nob, was with David; this meant that David now possessed the ephod, the sacred oracle, and was therefore in a position to consult Yahweh. In the present situation, for example, before setting out to follow the Amalekites it seemed wise to find out whether the counter-raid would be a success. The ephod indicated that it would; and so with a section of his men he took the road to the south. He had the good fortune to discover the robbers' tracks. Believing David to be away on a distant campaign, they had become careless about their own protection. *They were scattered over the whole countryside, eating, drinking and rejoicing*. David fell upon them, broke them, and began a systematic massacre. He recaptured all the prisoners and animals alive, took away a considerable quantity of war material, and went back to Ziklag a conqueror.

Out of his personal share of the booty taken from

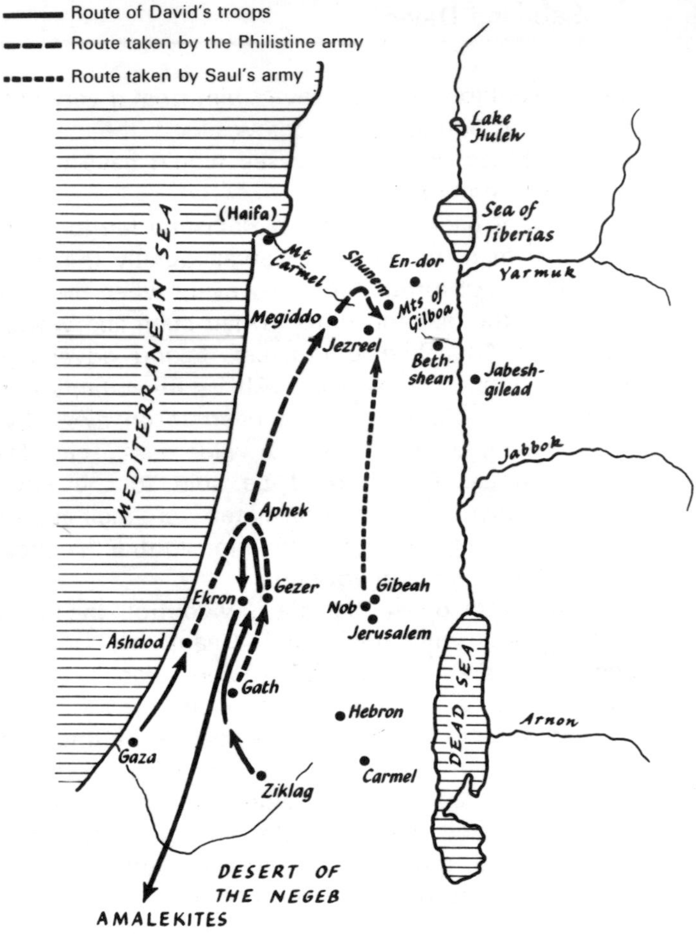

The Philistines decided to take the war against Israel into the fertile plain of Jezreel.

David, as vassal of the prince of Gath, goes up with the Philistine troops to fight against his Israelite brothers. Fortunately at Aphek (where all the troops gathered) he was thought to be an untrustworthy auxiliary and was sent back to Ziklag. His campaign in the south against the Amalekites.

At En-dor Saul consults the witch; his interview with Samuel's spirit. The battle at the foot of Gilboa. Death of Saul and three of his sons. Defeat of the Israelites.

these *enemies of Yahweh* – they were idolators and sworn foes of the Hebrews – he was careful to select a number of substantial gifts for the chieftains of Judah, the tribes of Caleb, Jerahmeel, Carmel, Hormah, Hebron, etc. He was an expert in public relations. *Thereupon his praises were widely proclaimed throughout Israel.* He had early been a renowned military leader, and in exile had shown himself very generous to his fellow-believers.

The position was briefly this: in the north, the tribes, exasperated by the moods of the unbalanced monarch, turned increasingly towards his former second-in-command. No one there had forgotten his striking victories, his countless triumphs. And yet now, through Saul's jealousy, he was a distant exile. He was Israel's obvious leader, although it was unsafe to say so openly. In the south, his homeland, the tribes looked to him with sympathy, admiration and gratitude.

Then, through a wholly unexpected prohibition, he had not been permitted by the Philistines to take part in their battle against Israel. He had thus been spared from taking part in an action which would have weighed heavily against him in the years ahead.

A major part of the country would therefore have been glad to see him. But Saul, the Lord's anointed, whom it was sacrilege to injure, still reigned, and the existence of his three sons seemed to make the future of his dynasty secure. Even so, David, for various reasons, was the chieftain whom many Hebrew leaders wanted as their leader.

Battle approaches

Meanwhile the two parties in the north – the Philistines and Israel – were preparing for battle. The Philistines had concentrated their forces at Aphek, and then moved forward to Shunem, on the far east of the plain of Jezreel. There they were joined by the Zekals, compatriots who had settled in the neighbourhood, by other settlers from the Aegean, and by neighbouring Canaanite princelings whose policy had always been the formation of a common front against the Hebrew newcomers. The latter, therefore, had to meet a coalition of some strength.

Saul left his capital Gibeah in great haste. By forced marches he advanced to the district between Jezreel and the Jordan, in order to obstruct the enemy's plan of campaign, which appeared to be aiming at Transjordania, with Damascus as its probable objective. He stopped first at Shunem, north of the city of Jezreel, but he was doubtful about an engagement, and took up a position close to Mount Gilboa. He realized that on the plain it would be impossible to withstand the onslaught of the Philistine armour. Israel's troops had only light equipment that made them chiefly effective in the hills, whereas the Philistines with their huge numbers, including chariots, a solid mass of infantry, and a mobile body of archers, would be a far more formidable army.

Saul's morale was already profoundly shaken. Morbid ideas obsessed him, and when he saw the Philistine camp his courage forsook him; all the more so, because of gloomy forebodings about the future. In the south, David his successor (if Samuel's obscure predictions were to be credited) was only waiting for his armies to be defeated in order to seize the throne. Saul was well aware that Yahweh, Israel's God, had forsaken him.

He ordered a consultation of the oracle. It remained silent. Anguish engulfed him. No one around him offered advice to encourage him. Then he said to his servants: *'Find a woman who is a necromancer for me to go and consult her.'* They replied that there was such a person near En-dor, a small township near to Mount Tabor.

Unfortunately, he had earlier issued a series of ruthless edicts against all the witches who, in one place or another, summoned up the dead, or claimed to read the future. This witch, therefore, must on no account recognize him. So, dressed as a soldier, he went to her, accompanied by two comrades, and said: *'Disclose the future to me by means of a ghost. Conjure up the one I shall name to you.'* She distrusted this unknown person and excused herself on the grounds of the king's prohibition, and asked: *'Why are you setting a trap for my life, to have me killed?'* Saul did not reveal himself, but he replied on oath that she had nothing to fear. At once she began her magic. *'Whom shall I conjure up for you?'* she inquired, and he replied: *'Samuel.'* Thereupon, she cried out: *'You are Saul.'* He calmed her as best he could, and demanded: *'What do you see?'* She was a medium, accustomed to calling up spirits of the dead; Scripture calls her: 'mistress of a spirit', in the Septuagint 'ventriloquist'. The scene was, in fact, one of traditional spiritualism: mediums, in their induced sleep, often altered their voices to become the expression of the being supposedly speaking through their mouths. The word 'ventriloquist' is to some extent an apt way of expressing the vocal changes which accompany in their messages.

It is worth noting that no form was visible to Saul during this seance. Only the witch was able to see and hear the dead person whose outward appearance she described, and whose words she uttered.

'I see a ghost rising up from the earth', she said. Saul asked her what he was like. *'It is an old man coming up'*, she answered, *'he is wrapped in his cloak'*.

Saul then knew it was Samuel, and he bowed to the ground. The ghost was still as unpleasant as when he was alive, and he began with severe reproaches against the man whom he had always rebuked. '*Why*', he complained, '*have you disturbed my rest, conjuring me up?*' Saul did his best to excuse himself; he explained that he was in great distress; the Philistines were on the verge of battle; divination had yielded no results; what was he to do? The prophet's answer was appalling: '*Why do you consult me when Yahweh has abandoned you and is with your neighbour? . . . He has snatched the sovereignty from your hand and given it to your neighbour, David, because you disobeyed the voice of Yahweh . . . That is why Yahweh treats you like this now . . . Yahweh will deliver Israel and you, too, into the power of the Philistines. Tomorrow you and your sons will be with me;*[15] *and Israel's army too, for Yahweh will deliver it into the power of the Philistines.*'

Saul was overcome and fell full length on the ground – he had eaten nothing on the previous day. When he recovered, both the witch and his own servants urged him to take a little food to get some strength for his journey. At first he refused, but in the end he gave way to their insistent requests. The witch owned a fattened calf which she quickly slaughtered. Then she took some flour, kneaded it, made cakes of unleavened bread, and baked them.

The battle of Gilboa and the death of Saul

Saul was beaten before he began. Scripture provides

[15] In Sheol, the common meeting place for the dead. At this period, there was no question about reward or punishment *after death*, for God had already bestowed happiness on the righteous and misery on the wicked during their lifetimes. This at least was the still hesitant theology of the Pentateuch, a very ancient and sometimes extremely primitive source. Only in the writings of the third and especially of the second century before Christ, do we find belief in the heavenly rewards of the believer and the punishments of the impious.

no details about the way the battle swayed. It simply says that the Hebrew defeat was total.

Saul's sons – Jonathan and two of his brothers – were among the first to fall. Saul had been obliged to fight a rearguard action, but the Philistine archery took him by surprise and wounded him seriously. He wanted at all costs to avoid capture and be gloated over, and he told his armour-bearer to take his sword and run him through with it. The man, a Hebrew, was afraid to do this terrible thing to the Lord's anointed. So Saul took his own sword and fell on it. His horrified armour-bearer followed his example. Israel's army, panic-stricken, was utterly defeated.

Next day, the victors came to strip the dead. On the slopes of Mount Gilboa they found the bodies of Saul and his three sons. They cut off the king's head, and sent his armour to Philistia, where they took it from city to city as a sign of good news to the idols and the people. It was then deposited in the temple of Astarte at Ashkelon, Astarte's chief sanctuary. Saul's head was fastened to the wall of Beth-shan. His sons were similarly treated. Travellers and caravans could thus see the mutilated bodies of Israel's leaders. The news of the Philistine victory would spread quickly.

The Israelite tribes on the other side of the Jordan learnt of this fearful disaster, although the Philistines do not seem to have pressed their advantage; it does not appear that they approached the river. Nevertheless fear reigned among the Israelites of Transjordania. The inhabitants of Jabesh-gilead, rescued by Saul in his first exploit as a young king, were deeply distressed at the mutilation of their benefactor's body. They marched secretly throughout the night and brought the bodies of Saul and his sons to Jabesh and burnt them there. This action is a little surprising in view of the Semitic horror of cremation. But it was really only a quick disposal of the flesh. The bones were preserved. This is confirmed by Scripture which says that after burning the bodies, *they took their bones and buried them under the tamarisk tree*.

An estimate of Saul's work

The failure of Israel's first king seems obvious. The unity of the Twelve Tribes under the aegis of Yahweh – indispensable if the Hebrew people and their spiritual message were to survive – had not yet been achieved. The Philistines and Canaanites still occupied large sections of the country. Desert bandits remained aggressive and daring. Palestine, the Promised Land, was still far from being under the control of Abraham's descendants. The fundamental hopes that had filled the heart of Israel from Joshua to the Judges, were now only sad and nostalgic memories. When Saul fell on his sword at Gilboa to escape from the Philistines, he left behind him a situation that seemed desperate. In reality it was not so. With Saul's death a dead star had vanished in the north. But in the south, among the mountains of Judah, a new star, David, was shining.

5

KING DAVID (1010–970)

While these events were taking place on the slopes of Gilboa, David, the petty chieftain, the vassal of the Philistines, had just returned to his dwelling at Ziklag after the counter-raid on the Amalekites. He possessed too keen a political sense not to realize that, one way or another, it was his own political destiny that was at stake on the plain of Jezreel in the encounter between the Philistines and the Israelite army of Saul.

David learns of the death of Saul

For two days David and his band of adventurers had been back in the ruins of their burnt-out city. On the third day a messenger appeared, a man with torn garments, his head covered with dust, who had come by forced marches from Gilboa. He brought the latest news of the battle: it was a complete victory for the Philistines. The Israelite army had been routed, and Saul was dead together with his three sons who were with him. Untruthfully, the messenger asserted that he himself had struck down his sovereign since Saul did not wish to fall alive into the hands of the enemy. As proof of his assertion he handed David the crown and bracelet[1] belonging to Saul. *'And I have brought*

[1] The crown: little is known about the shape of this royal emblem (nezer); the Hebrew word suggests the idea of consecration. Was it a circlet worn round the forehead or just a golden flower? Bracelet: it appears that men wore it above the elbow; it should be regarded as a military emblem.

them here to my Lord,' concluded the messenger, confidently awaiting his reward.

David began by tearing his garments as a sign of mourning. His soldiers followed his example. From all sides rose lamentations, weeping and the wailing of despair. A few moments later David turned to this messenger who prided himself on having struck down Saul when he begged to be killed. *'How is it,'* he asked, *'you were not afraid to lift your hand to destroy Yahweh's anointed?'* And he ordered one of his soldiers to strike the man down.

There can be no doubt of David's respectful attitude to the king. On several occasions we have seen that he could easily have killed Saul who was persecuting him so harshly, but he was careful not to commit this sacrilege; indeed in the cave of Engedi, as on the Hill of Hachilah, David prevented his comrades in arms from killing Saul when he was within their grasp. It was quite logical therefore on his part to condemn the king's murderer, but this should not prevent our noting David's great political skill as well; he was certainly well aware of the implications of his action and its bearing on the future.

David's Elegy on Saul and the dead on Gilboa (2 Sam. 1: 17–27)

At once David began to chant the famous lament. Philologists regard it as a composition contemporary with the battle of Gilboa; in addition it bears every mark of being inspired by David. *It is written in the Book of the Just,* an ancient collection of poems to which the writer refers from time to time, *so that it may be taught to the sons of Judah* (2 Sam. 1: 18).

The following extracts from the poem give some idea of its lofty inspiration and stirring emotion. Orientalists regard it as one of the purest gems of Hebrew poetry.

Alas, the glory of Israel has been slain on your heights!
How did the heroes fall?

The 'glory of Israel' refers to Saul and Jonathan, 'the flower, the beauty, the pride' of Israel.

Do not speak of it in Gath,
nor announce it in the streets of Ashkelon,
or the daughters of the Philistines will rejoice,
the daughters of the uncircumcized will gloat.

Gath and Ashkelon were cities of the Philistine territory of Pentapolis. Generally it was the women who celebrated the exploits of the warriors in songs and dances to the sound of the tambourine. (We have already encountered this in the chapter devoted to Jephthah.)

O mountains of Gilboa,
let there be no dew or rain on you;
treacherous fields,
for there the hero's shield was dishonoured!

Dew, rain: when in this very chalky land of Canaan the grass and cultivated land did not have enough rain it was an agricultural disaster. To wish drought on a country meant asking for its ruin.

The shield of Saul was anointed not with oil
but with blood of the wounded, fat of the warriors;
the bow of Jonathan did not turn back,
nor the sword of Saul return idle.
Saul and Jonathan, loved and lovely,
neither in life, nor in death, were divided.
Swifter than eagles were they,
stronger were they than lions.

In his song in praise of the heroes of Israel, David does not separate his faithful and affectionate friend Jonathan, Saul's son, from Saul himself, the old king who had pursued him with his bitter hatred for years. There is always this respect for the 'Lord's anointed'.

O daughters of Israel, weep for Saul
who clothed you in scarlet and fine linen,
who set brooches of gold
on your garments.

This is characteristically oriental; it recalls the sharing out of the booty after a raid; the women were not forgotten. Garments and jewels brought back from an expedition formed the share of wives and daughters from the triumphant soldiers.

How did the heroes fall
in the thick of battle?

The interrogative form used by the poet, and it recurs in this piece, is still used in Arabic elegies nowadays.

O Jonathan, in your death I am stricken,
I am desolate for you, Jonathan my brother.

This is pure lyrical poetry, a cry from the very depths of the soul. It will be noticed that throughout the piece there is an entire absence of the religious motive; the name of Yahweh is not even uttered. It is a lament that is intended to remain on the human level.

How did the heroes fall
and the battle armour fail?

David decides to return to the land of Yahweh

David was an inspired poet, but he was also certainly a political realist. After mourning Saul, he felt that it was time to take possession of his inheritance without delay, at least of the nearby southern territories (Judah,

Simeon and various groups which were vaguely Yahwist).

He could be fairly certain of receiving a welcome from these southern peoples. In the first place, he himself was from Judah. In addition, as has been pointed out, he had been clever enough to ally himself by several marriages to the powerful tribe of Caleb whose chieftains lived at Hebron, the ancient religious centre of the south. Then, throughout the south, not only had David while employed by the Philistines, refrained from laying waste his co-religionists' territory, but he had even sent them a share in the booty captured in battle from the Amalekite nomads of the desert, the avowed enemies of the Israelites. In addition, his exploits were famous throughout Judah. He had only to appear for the whole country to come out on his side – or at least, so he hoped.

David becomes the 'Lord's anointed', 1010 (2 Sam. 2)

Devout, and artful, as always, David consulted the oracle through the intermediary of Abiathar the priest. '*Shall I go up to one of the towns of Judah?*' he asked. '*Go up,*' came the answer. Further question: '*Which shall I go to?*' '*To Hebron,*' came the answer.

The order came from Yahweh and there could be no avoiding it; on the other hand, victory was assured. So David hastened to leave the Philistine territory of Ziklag and returned at last to the land of his fathers. With his wives he settled at Hebron. His men at arms, always ready to take action against any foe on a signal from their leader, established themselves in the same city or in the immediate neighbourhood. There was no hostile reaction in the country, quite the contrary in fact: there at Hebron *the men of Judah came and anointed David king over the House of Judah*. He was a young king, for at that time he was scarcely thirty years old.

Ishbaal, son of Saul, made king over Israel

Up in the north, Abner, Saul's army commander, defeated at Gilboa, was obliged to cross the Jordan to escape the continuing pressure from the Philistines; with what remained of his troops he settled at Mahanaim (the Two Camps) on the left bank of the river. We have already encountered this place in the story of Jacob. Abner took with him Ishbaal, one of Saul's sons, providentially saved from the slaughter. And there in Transjordania, *Ishbaal son of Saul was forty years old when he became king of Israel*.

Thus while David made a triumphant return to the Promised Land to be proclaimed king of Judah, Ishbaal, the real heir of the dead king, was obliged to flee to the other side of the Jordan to be an exiled king.

Formation of the two kingdoms, Judah and Israel
(see map, p. 111)

Thus the Promised Land was unfortunately divided into two 'kingdoms'. The political unity which Saul had tried to establish had certainly appeared very precarious. But it was far better than this clear-cut division. There were two kingdoms: Israel (in the north), Judah (in the south). There were two kings: Ishbaal, son of Saul, king of Israel; David, the former shepherd from Bethlehem, the outlaw and guerilla fighter, king of Judah.

So far the word Israel has been used to designate the Twelve Tribes as a whole. Israel ('God is strong') was the new name given to Jacob by Yahweh at the crossing of the Jabbok; and each of the twelve Hebrew tribes bore the name of one of the twelve descendants of the patriarch Jacob-Israel.

From this point onwards we shall be unable to use

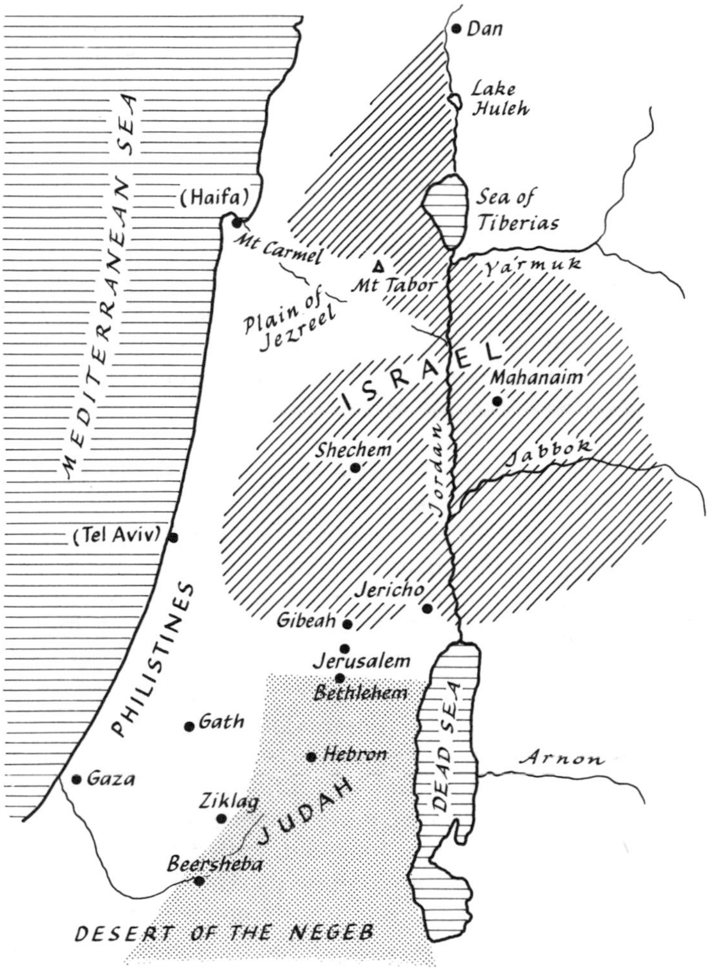

Territory of the kingdom of Israel. Capital, Mahanaim. King: Ishbaal.

Territory of the kingdom of Judah: Capital, Hebron. King, David.

Between the two kingdoms, the citadel of Urushalim (Jerusalem).

1010–1003: THE TWO HEBREW KINGDOMS: ISRAEL AND JUDAH

the same terms as hitherto owing to the political change brought about by the coronation of David. Despite certain temporary unifications, from that time two geographical and political groups were to be distinguished: in the centre and in the north, Israel (ten tribes: Benjamin, Dan, Ephraim, Manasseh, Issachar, Zebulun, Asher, Naphtali, Gad and Reuben); to the south, Judah (combining the two tribes of Judah and Simeon to which were joined a certain number of clans of Yahwist tendencies). After 1010, therefore, these two terms must be distinguished, and Israel no longer designates the Chosen People as a whole.

Here must be added a short word about Judah.

Morally and religiously it formed a clear contrast with Israel. These southern settlements, cut off from their northern co-religionists by the Canaanite enclave of Urushalim (Jerusalem), developed on their own and in a somewhat different way. In this part of the country the tribes of Simeon and Judah were allied with the Calebites, men of their own race;[2] and also with tribes of Edomite origin (descendants of Kenaz, Jerahmeel, Cain, etc). In short, David had grouped around him two tiny Hebrew tribes (Judah and Simeon) swollen by numerous Canaanite elements, recently assimilated, among which were included settled farmers, of course, but also wandering shepherds. Under the guidance of its new head this new state soon became a populous, rich kingdom, remarkable for its political stability. In addition, under David's influence it began to appear as

[2] It is very probable that the Calebites were Yahwist groups which, wandering on the plains of Sinai under Moses' leadership, with all the other Israelite forces gathered at Kadesh, went out to attack Canaan to the south. But, unlike their companions in arms, the Calebites seem to have broken through the lines of the southern Canaanites, and settled down at Hormah. The greater part of Moses' troops, on the other hand, were obliged to retreat on Kadesh. See volume *Moses* in this series, p. 140, with geographical sketch, pp. 138–139.

the centre of Yahwism, a choice field for the deepening of the religious consciousness of the Chosen People.

Fratricidal wars between the two kingdoms (1010–1003, approximate dates)

The Hebrew people were divided into two kingdoms each under the leadership of a different king. The inevitable consequence was war.

For seven years (1010–1003), from the battle of Gilboa onwards, the two kingdoms were to be in bitter opposition, always at each other's throats and killing each other. Thus during a guerilla engagement Abner, Saul's former general, kept in office by Ishbaal, killed the brother of Joab, David's general, and a vendetta was added to the military rivalry of the leaders of the opposing armies.

This war of attrition was by no means to David's liking; he was far too intelligent not to deplore this state of affairs – though it must be admitted that it was he who had provoked it. After all, it would have been easy enough for him to have offered his sword as commander-in-chief to Ishbaal, the legitimate king. But David was ambitious. The tiny kingdom of Judah was not enough for him and he looked towards the northern federation of tribes. And all the more since he realized that his opponent Ishbaal was a puppet in the hands of Abner, his general. David felt called to wear both crowns, and suddenly the opportunity came through two unforeseen circumstances.

Death of Abner (2 Sam. 3: 12–27)

Abner, Saul's former general and his cousin, was a good tactician and energetic and intelligent; in addition, he was an astute diplomat. His eminent military qualities quickly enabled him to retrieve from the Philistines, who were victorious at Gilboa, a great part of the territory lost by Saul. But he was fully aware that Ishbaal, his king, was not of the same calibre as David, a leader of genius. In short, Abner decided to abandon his own sovereign and to tie up his fortunes with those of the king of Judah. It should be added that Abner had fallen out with Ishbaal over a concubine. Abner began secret diplomatic conversations between Mahanaim (the capital of Israel) and Hebron (the capital of Judah). Abner had succeeded in circumventing some of the influential chieftains of the northern tribes; he put it around that the frightful fratricidal war could not last much longer and that the indispensable solution was to place David at the head of a unified kingdom. The unfortunate Ishbaal's opinion was not asked and he seems to have been kept in ignorance of the whole business.

Before going further in the matter David demanded that his Benjamite wife, Michal, Saul's daughter, should be returned to him. Saul had given her to him for his wife and then had taken her back after the affair of the teraphim in the bed (1 Sam. 19: 13–17). To punish both accomplices in the trick played upon him Saul had given Michal in marriage to a somewhat obscure figure, Palti or Paltiel, son of Laish. By thus regaining the daughter of the dead king, David might claim rights over the kingdom of Saul, his former father-in-law. Once more, Ishbaal's authorization was not asked. Abner took it upon himself to restore Michal to her former husband. Paltiel, in tears, followed the procession. At the frontier between Benjamin and Judah, Abner said to him '*Go back,*' and he went.

Abner pursued the matter briskly. He explained his plan for a union of the two kingdoms, and assured David that Israel was ready to throw in its lot with him. All seemed set for success. Accompanied by twenty men, Abner accepted David's invitation to come to Hebron. A banquet was held to celebrate in proper fashion the end of the hostilities and the reunification of the kingdom. All seemed settled for the best. But there was still Joab.

Joab was David's general and also his nephew (by his mother Zeruiah, David's sister), and the brother of Asahel who was killed in battle by Abner. Joab was a first-class military leader and entirely devoted to his uncle. He was a rough, brutal and merciless creature, jealous of his own authority. He regarded the agreement between David and Abner very unfavourably, since he considered the latter as a worthless soldier. If the union of Israel and Judah were ever to take place Abner's position would be at the head of the Yahwist armies, which Joab himself had counted on occupying. The rivalry between the two men seemed certain to come to a head before very long. Joab, a determined man, quickly found a solution.

Since Abner had killed Joab's brother, Joab had become for this reason his brother's *go'el*, the avenger of his blood. Among the Hebrews a father's blood had to be avenged by his son, a brother's blood by his brother, or failing these, by the nearest relation. Consequently, Asahel's avenger would be one of his two brothers, Joab or Abishai. Abner needed to be on his guard.

After the banquet given him by David at Hebron, Abner took leave of the king and prepared to return to the north to work for the effective reunion of the two kingdoms. Directly after his departure Joab arrived. He was returning from a raid against the nomad tribes and brought back with him rich plunder for the community. Only then did he learn of the visit of his military rival, Abner. Suspecting that Abner had been negotiating for the supreme command of the army, Joab became very angry and made a great scene with his uncle David. *'Do you not know Abner, son of Ner?'* he cried. *'He came to trick you, to know your every move, to find out what you are doing.'* David knew his nephew's violent temper and let him have his say.

Joab was a realist. He lost no time and, unknown to David, sent a messenger to request Abner to return immediately. Thinking that the king wished to give him further instructions Abner turned back. At the gate of Hebron Joab awaited him; he led him aside, as if to speak to him privately. *And there*, says the Bible, *he struck him in the belly, and so, for the blood of Joab's brother Asahel, he died*.

Despite its apparent legality such an execution at this time was very awkward indeed. David might well be suspected of the murder of Abner, since his death would to some extent favour David's plans; he would be in a position to dictate his conditions to the chieftains of Mahanaim since there was now no commander on Ishbaal's side capable of opposing Joab successfully.

Obviously it was important that the king of Judah should not be suspected of murder or even of complicity, so David took particular care to proclaim his anger, to show his disapproval and to swear that he was absolutely innocent of this crime. 'May the blood of Abner,' he solemnly announced, 'fall on the head of Joab and his family!' He ordered the leading persons of his court (among whom was Joab) to put on sackcloth as a sign of mourning. In addition, David led the mourning; he walked in the first place behind the bier and at the moment of burial he wept aloud. Then the king gave way to the poet and he began to sing this lament:

> *'Should Abner have died as a fool dies?*
> *Your hands were not tied, your feet not chained;*
> *you fell as a man falls at the hands of criminals.'*[3]

After the funeral ceremony David was invited to take some food. David ostentatiously refused. *That day all the people of Judah and all Israel understood that the king had no part in the death of Abner son of Ner*. The relations of the dead man, too, were quite convinced that David was innocent. Negotiations continued normally between them and the king and an agreement was soon reached.

It was true nonetheless that Abner's death was a fortunate occurrence for David. Abner had prepared the way for David to obtain the Israelite crown. But if Abner had continued to live it would only have complicated the situation. He was full of ambition and he was artful, cunning and unscrupulous. David could have expected to pay dearly for the great service rendered to him.

Death of Ishbaal (2 Sam. 4)

In this sombre story Ishbaal, son of Saul, the legitimate king of Israel, seems almost to have been forgotten; but he had no intention of standing aside for his southern rival. The Israelite soldiers, however, were unwilling to continue the struggle against David and even preferred to serve under his command.

[3] We probably possess only a fragment of the lament. The words are to be understood as follows: Abner was struck down by a sudden death; this is usually reserved to the wicked (the punishment of heaven). He was struck down (wrongly, of course) like a criminal (punishment of men). He did not enjoy, unfortunately, the death that he merited, namely, death in battle.

Increasingly, as the days went by, Ishbaal felt himself isolated and abandoned by all.

Among Ishbaal's officers were *two freebooting chieftains*, rough and primitive characters, called Baanah and Rechab. In their opinion the required solution was simple: if they killed their sovereign the political problem would be solved. At the hottest part of the day, when everyone took a siesta, they went to the door of Ishbaal's house at Mahanaim. The woman who kept the door had been cleaning wheat and she had drowsed off to sleep in the heat. Rechab and Baanah stole into the house and went straight to Ishbaal's room, surprised the king while he was asleep and without more ado ran him through with a sword. After which they cut off his head. Taking the head, they set off along the valley of the Jordan, travelling throughout the night; in the morning they arrived at Hebron, asked to be received by David and triumphantly presented him with the head of his rival. The murderers expected to receive a reward worthy of their exploit. But David was shocked by their deed, and in addition he was an astute diplomat; he realized that he must not be suspected in the slightest degree of any complicity in this sordid affair. The harsh words that he addressed to the murderers left them in no doubt: *'The man who thought to bring me good news when he told me Saul was dead, this man I seized and killed at Ziklag, rewarding him for his good news!'* He made a sign to the guards which they understood at once. The two Benjamite chieftains fell beneath the blows of the soldiers. Their hands and feet were cut off and their corpses hung up on a tree near the Pool of Hebron.

David had Ishbaal's head buried with great ceremony in Abner's tomb. Both by his attitude and by the various measures which he publicly adopted he wished to prove that he had had nothing to do with the murder of the king of Israel. From the evidence available about the murders of Abner and Ishbaal it does seem that David was innocent of the blood of these two men. Quite simply events worked in his favour. After this the crown of Israel could not be long in coming his way.

David, king of Judah and of Israel

The feeling caused by these two murders soon calmed down. The chieftains of Mahanaim, already influenced by Abner's policy, looked towards Hebron; the turn of events seemed increasingly favourable to realization of the unity of the Twelve Tribes.

Save for Meribbaal, Jonathan's son, who was lame and deformed, the royal house of Saul was practically speaking no longer in existence (or at least so it was thought).

The royal house of Judah was far better placed with David, Saul's former military leader, and the hero of a hundred battles against the Philistines. In the camps the soldiers recounted the warrior's mighty deeds, embellishing them, as was only to be expected. In the villages the storytellers entertained the people with David's exploits. In short, throughout the land there was a popular movement, backed up by a powerful political party supported by the leaders of the army and by religious circles, demanding that David should be acknowledged as king of all the Hebrews. Logic required it: the two crowns of Israel and Judah should be reunited on the head of the leader who dwelt at Hebron. Only at this price could the People of God be saved from the ever-threatening peril from the Philistines and, by the same token, be delivered from all danger of separatism.

And so it was that one of the Israelite chieftains from Mahanaim, accompanied by soldiers, went to Hebron. There, in true eastern fashion, long and verbose negotiations took place. The golden ingots from David's treasury no doubt played their part. Finally, in the sanctuary at Hebron, *in the presence of Yahweh* the solemn pact was concluded and David received the anointing with sacred oil which made him king of Israel and of Judah.

David was the 'Lord's anointed'. The word 'anointed' is 'Messiah' in Hebrew and 'Christ' in Greek. These two last terms, at first synonyms of 'appointed king', were subsequently applied to the Chosen People as a whole. Later they were reserved for certain prophets endued with a mission of consolation and hope. Then they were used of the 'Liberator' who was foretold and awaited. Lastly, they were applied to Jesus of Nazareth and to him alone.

David, who was already king of Judah, had now become king of Israel. Henceforward he was to reign over the Twelve Tribes. The herdsman of Bethlehem, in charge of his father's sheep, was now the sovereign of the People of God. He had come a long way.

This success was bound to cause serious concern to the Philistines. At one moment they had thought that the two kingdoms of Judah and Israel, separated and at variance, would come into conflict and destroy each other. The master-stroke by David, their former vassal, took them by surprise. They decided at once on counter measures.

David puts an end to the Philistine danger

The Philistines attacked. They deployed their troops in the country south of Jerusalem, a stronghold still in the hands of the Jebusites, a Canaanite tribe. It was obvious that their objective was to cut the forces of Israel and Judah in two.

David replied by a guerilla action. The struggle was sharp and David was not successful on all occasions. The Philistine troops laid waste the north of Judah. In return the Hebrews launched attacks right into Philistia. David, the popular leader whose orders were obeyed with enthusiasm, had formations of seasoned troops who fought relentlessly and were increasingly successful, even to the point that the final, definitive victory could be foreseen.

The Bible mentions two pitched battles, both of which took place in the valley of Rephaim, close to Jerusalem. During the first of these encounters not only did David succeed in throwing back the enemy to their starting-point, but he seized the Philistine idols which their leaders had been imprudent enough to bring on to the battlefield in order to be assured of their protection. David burnt them. During the second action David pursued the enemy as far as the neighbourhood of Gezer. This enabled the troops of Yahweh to penetrate into the richest part of Philistia, the coastal region and the cultivated plains of Sharon and Shephelah. Although in this passage of the Bible the text is in a poor state and is difficult to interpret, it seems probable that David's army even seized the Philistine citadel of Gath, the stronghold governed by Achish, the chieftain of the Peoples of the Sea whose vassal David had been at the time of his exile. Times had changed indeed.

At that time the cities in the north (on the plain of Jezreel) occupied by, or in subjection to, the Philistines were incorporated into the Hebrew kingdom. It was victory all along the line. By his methodical application of a bold plan David swiftly succeeded in eliminating the Philistine peril which had been a source of anxiety for two centuries.

King David in his capital Hebron (2 Sam. 2: 2–4; 3: 2–5)

The new king could look on his achievements with some satisfaction. He had settled in Hebron, his capital, with his military court; in the neighbourhood of this small city his troops were encamped under the command of chieftains who were entirely devoted to him. He had also his harem; this was a royal prerogative. His firstborn was Amnon, by Ahinoam. His second son was Chileab by the beautiful Abigail from Carmel. The third was Absalom whose mother was Maacah. The fourth son was Adonijah, and the fifth and sixth were Shephatiah and Ithream. This encouraging start for the royal lineage at Hebron sufficed to ensure the future of the dynasty, but David's descendants were not confined to these children; at Jerusalem, a little later, the family circle continued to increase.

On the political level the two great objectives of the Hebrews, close centralization of the Twelve Tribes and elimination of the Philistine danger, had now been attained.

On the religious level the kingdom of Israel-Judah could congratulate itself on possessing a devout king, who would not follow in the footsteps of his predecessor Saul. The Chosen People felt heartened; their sovereign was convinced that the salvation of the House of Jacob was not to be found in the mere ambition of its leaders but in observance of the law of God.

David chooses a new capital: Jerusalem

Despite its unification the Hebrew kingdom continued to possess two capitals: Mahanaim in Transjordania and Hebron in Judah.

David, having rendered the Philistine war machine powerless, began to consider where best to have his capital city, because neither Mahanaim nor Hebron was really suitable.

From the political point of view it was impossible to give preference to either city, at least if peace was to be maintained between the two parts of the kingdom. To make Mahanaim the capital would mean provoking the general reprobation of David's bands of warriors who, for the most part, belonged to the south. To remain at Hebron would mean causing an affront to the quarrelsome chieftains of the northern tribes. The young king, desiring to obtain the support of all by a wise policy, contrived to avoid petty differences of this kind.

From the administrative and military point of view the two capitals had a serious disadvantage: they were both situated in frontier regions. Of course, the capital could have been established once more at Gibeah of Benjamin, Saul's royal seat, but David was too clever to renew in one way or another any connection with the extinct dynasty. What he required was a city entirely independent of the history of the Hebrews, a neutral territory, a new setting in which the new king would be really in his own place.

David was thoroughly acquainted with this region. As a fugitive, an underground fighter and an adept at guerilla warfare, he had travelled over the whole of this countryside in all directions. Thus he was able to decide very quickly: he would make Jerusalem his capital city. It was an old Semitic city, named Urushalim, occupied at that time by a Canaanite clan called the Jebusites.

In addition, if he could obtain possession of Jerusalem he would abolish the partition unfortunately separating

Israel in the north from Judah in the south. Ever since the time of Joshua this Canaanite fortress had always proved an obstacle to relations between the tribes in the south and the northern federation. If Jerusalem had not entirely isolated the two divisions of the Hebrew people from each other, it at least proved a considerable hindrance to cultural exchanges, thus encouraging the development of differing interpretations of Yahwism.

The matter then was definitely decided upon; it seemed absolutely necessary for David to establish his capital in Jerusalem. The only difficulty was that Jerusalem was in the hands of the Canaanites.

Jerusalem, Jebus, City of David, Zion, Ophel (see plan, p. 128)

So far Jerusalem has hardly been mentioned in the Bible owing to the fact that the Hebrews always avoided this place because it was held to be impregnable. Before examining its geographical situation, we must consider the subject of its name, or rather the names given to it by the ancient chroniclers and also the modern historians – Jerusalem, Jebus, Ophel, City of David, Zion – certainly requires some explanation.

It has now been clearly established that from the first half of the second millenium, the probable date of its historical foundation,[4] according to the findings of the archaeologists, the city was called Urushalim – 'foundation of Salem', the 'city ('ir) of Salem', Salem (or Shalom) being a god venerated in the Amorite (Canaanite) religion; it was a deity of universalist character (but not the one God); the Semites of this region called it 'the Most High', the 'creator of heaven

[4] Before the historical foundation of the city prehistoric peoples occupied the place.

David with all Israel marched on Jerusalem . . . David went to live in the fortress, and that is how it came to be called the Citadel of David . . . David grew greater and greater, and Yahweh Sabaoth was with him.

1 Chron. 11 : 4–9

and earth'. We have already seen (cf. *Abraham*, pp. 109–110) that Melchizedek, king of Salem, at his meeting with Abraham, blessed the patriarch in the name of this god and that Abraham may well have thought it to be the one God with whose revelation he had previously been favoured. Thus from its historical origins until the time of Joshua the city bore the name of Urushalim, from which we have made 'Jerusalem'.

In the Bible we find it sometimes designated by the name Jebus. Now it was only in about 300 B.C. that the author of the Book of Chronicles thought of calling it Jebus from the fact that before David's time the city was inhabited by the Jebusites. In fact, Urushalim (Jerusalem) never changed its name after the beginning of the historical period (1 Chron. 11: 4).

We shall see in a moment why David, following an eastern custom but also, and chiefly, in pursuance of a clever political idea, called his conquest 'the city of David'. But, despite the new name given to it, Jerusalem was still the name in common use.

What was the reason for the name Zion, which occurs in some biblical passages and which has been used by some modern poets? Originally the name Zion (its etymology is doubtful) seems to have designated the Canaanite citadel established to the north of the rock to defend the city. Then, by extension, it came to designate the whole city; at a still later period it was used for the Temple raised up by Solomon to Yahweh on the northern terrace of the rocky plateau. Thus we can say that the expression Mount Zion is correctly used to designate the rocky hill of Jerusalem.[5]

[5] Here may be mentioned the topographical error made by the writers of the fourth century B.C. who gave the name of Zion to the high hill (2882 feet) rising to the west of the rock on the other side of the Tyropoeon Valley. This hill, included within the modern Jerusalem, has no right to the title that was given it,

The rock is also sometimes called Ophel (the hump, the hill): this was a popular and very ancient name.

Therefore, with some reservations on very small matters of detail, all these historical or geographical designations – Ophel, Urushalim (Jerusalem), Jebus City of David, Zion – can be regarded as equivalent terms.

The curious rocky spur Urushalim (see plan, p. 128)

A rapid glance at the topography of Jebusite Jerusalem (which was soon to become David's) is here necessary, to understand how the Canaanite stronghold, which was reputed to be impregnable, fell so rapidly into the hands of David.

The spur of limestone (V-shaped, with the apex at the southern end) on which, a little later, Solomon was to build the celebrated Temple of Yahweh, was bordered on each of its sides as follows:

To the east lies the deep ravine of the Kidron (at the bottom of which ran a small mountain stream flowing into the Dead Sea). On this side, on account of the difference of level (about 150 feet) between the fortified terrace and the bottom of the ravine, any idea of scaling the walls was out of the question.

To the west, by the Tyropoeon Valley, the same observation applies; the natural defences, reinforced by ramparts and towers, were ample discouragement to any attempt to take it by assault.

To the north, unfortunately, there was no natural defence, since the upper part of the V opened on the same level on to the mountain mass. Thus, from the bronze age onwards the occupants of the Ophel gave

even in the last century, of the 'Holy Mountain', although it contains several holy places, like the Holy Sepulchre, the Cenacle etc.

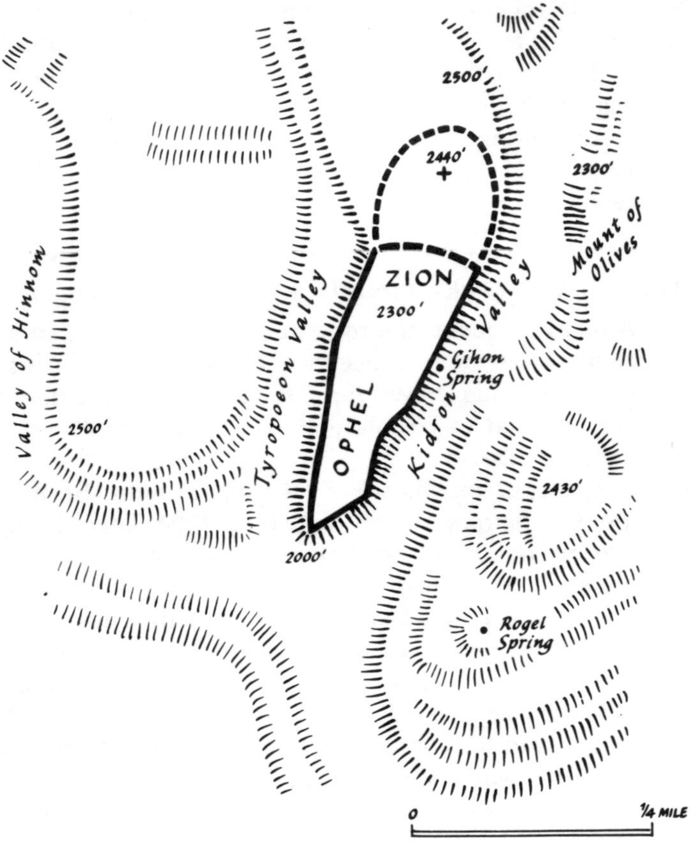

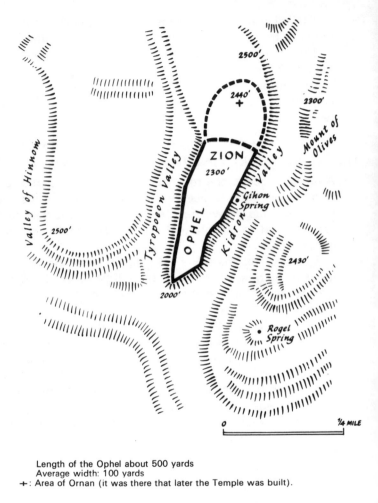

Length of the Ophel about 500 yards
Average width: 100 yards
+: Area of Ornan (it was there that later the Temple was built).

The URUSHALIM (JERUSALEM) of David also called OPHEL, ZION, or the CITY OF DAVID

special attention to fortifications on this the weak side of their rock, constructing ramparts, trenches and fortifications. At an early period a citadel (Zion) was built on this side.

All things considered, with the two steep valleys to the east and the west, strengthened by ramparts, bastions and the lines of fortifications on the north, it will be understood that in David's time Urushalim could be regarded as a stronghold defying any attack.

It may be wondered why the city had been established on the tiny hill of Ophel, when on the other side of the Tyropoeon Valley there was a much larger hill available (it was later the site of the Upper city of Jerusalem) with natural defences equal to those of the Ophel. The reason for the choice was very simple; at its lower end Ophel possessed a spring. In ancient times it was the water supply which governed the construction of fortresses; in case of siege, which might continue for years, the garrison required a supply of drinking water. Without a spring no military establishment was possible. A rock with a spring nearby was soon occupied by a city encircled with thick walls behind which the citizens could snap their fingers at the enemy.

The cave in which this spring rose beneath Ophel, and still more the passage giving access to the spring, were to play a leading part in the capture of the city by David. The spring was called Gihon.[6]

Unfortunately it could not be included within the

[6] Gihon, 'the spring' in Hebrew.'The only perpetual spring of water in Jerusalem', says Tacitus (*Historia* V, 12). It is of the type which gives water at regular intervals. Obviously it has remained at its primitive level, while the valley of the Kidron has been raised considerably in the course of centuries since the city disposed of its waste and rubbish there. Thus nowadays it is necessary to go down a flight of thirty stone steps (whence the present name of the spring 'the Mother of Steps') to get to the fresh water. The popular name 'Fountain of the Virgin' which has been given to it has no historical foundation.

fortifications of Jerusalem. This difficulty was overcome by the clever architects of the first Iron Age (1200–900 B.C. – that is, roughly the historical period of the Judges) who excavated a long tunnel, about a hundred feet long dropping over its whole length about 160 feet, in order to reach the spring under cover. To hide the source of the stream from possible assailants the entrance of the little cave had been built up and was thus out of sight of prying eyes. And so the fortress always possessed its supply of water.[7]

David lays siege to Jerusalem

David's plan was a bold one, the more so because, in fact, both politically and militarily, he could not afford a defeat. To associate the Hebrews as a whole in his victory David took care to besiege Jerusalem 'with all Israel', that is, with the warriors of all the tribes. Thus, at a later period 'all Israel' could boast of having taken part in the conquest of the capital.

And so the Hebrew army settled down around the stronghold to begin the siege. In accordance with ancient custom the Jebusites on top of the ramparts shouted all sorts of insults at their presumptuous opponents. *'You shall not enter here'* (1 Chron. 11: 5), they cried from the towers when they perceived David. And to emphasize the impregnable nature of the natural and artificial defences of the place they added: *'The blind and the lame will hold you off'* (2 Sam. 5: 6). They could hardly have shown themselves more confident.

[7] This secret underground passage is called in the Bible Zinnor (canal, small stream). This term has been adopted by the archaeologists to designate the tunnels of the same sort and of approximately the same period driven at the foot of certain citadels: Gezer and Megiddo.

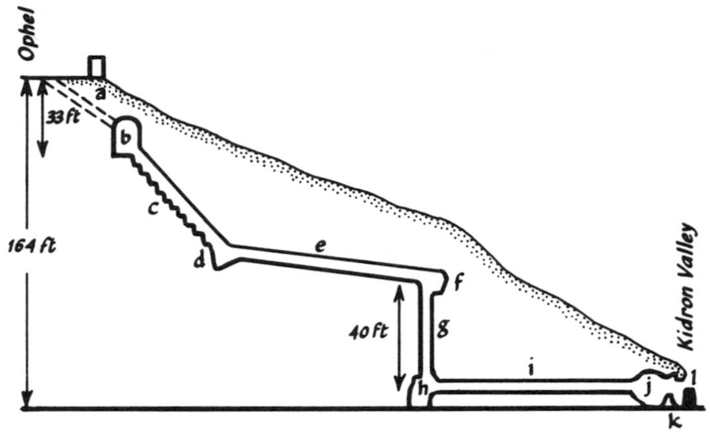

Diagram showing arrangement of the Zinnor of Jerusalem

- **a** Tunnel giving access to vaulted chamber (this way down has not yet been discovered).
- **b** Vaulted chamber at a depth of about 30 feet below the level of the Ophel. The vaulting is of a late period.
- **c** Steps cut in the rock, rather steep (30°).
- **d** Drop of about 8 feet, for which a ladder was probably used.
- **e** Slightly sloping gallery (7°).
- **f** Chamber with well into which water-drawers let down their water skins by ropes.
- **g** Vertical chimney, height 40 feet through which water was drawn up.
- **h** Cave used as a tank.
- **i** Channel taking the water from **j** to **h**.
- **k** The spring of Gihon.
- **l** Low wall, forming a dyke intended to direct water towards **h** through **l** instead of letting it flow direct into the Kidron.

The second Book of Samuel (5: 6–8) and the first Book of Chronicles (1: 4–7) unfortunately give only a short summary of operations whose details it would have been interesting to know. We are merely told that the siege threatened to be very long because any frontal attack would have proved very costly. On the other hand the Jebusites, who were well supplied with food and had plenty of water from the spring, could laugh at David's plans. And after all, even though he was thoroughly at home with all the tricks of an armed raid he was an absolute novice in everything to do with the operations of a siege. According to the account in the Bible it appears that the siege dragged on. David endeavoured to put new spirit into his men; he had it proclaimed throughout the camp that the first to strike down a Jebusite should become a leader and commander. Although in this chapter the text is very corrupt, this must be the moment when the initiative was seized by Joab (David's nephew and general; we have already encountered him here as the murderer of Abner). By means of a trick, with a handful of men, he contrived to seize the city.

Joab's exploit (see sketch, p. 131)

There were only two ways of capturing the citadel: surprise or treachery. We shall see how David used the first method, and possibly the second as well.

Over-confident in the inaccessibility of the underground tunnel leading to the spring, the Jebusites took little care over their defences on this side; watch over the tunnel by soldiers had been given up. Joab turned to good account this failure in military precautions.

It may be wondered how the place where the spring gushed forth (hidden by masonry) could have been known by the Hebrews. It is possible that before the seige a study of the terrain had been carried out by Israelite spies. It is also possible that the assailants' attention was drawn to the spring by the sound of voices or by the noise of the water itself echoing the underground galleries. Or the plan of the Zinnor may have been provided by a Jebusite traitor.

Joab, as we know, was a tough soldier, always ready for a daring exploit. Once the entry to the tunnel had been discovered, Joab and a handful of men secretly crept into the long horizontal gallery (marked **i** on the plan, p. 131) where the beseiged garrison had negligently omitted to post a sentry. Thus the raiders were able to advance along the gallery quite freely. In order to dig out the canal the builder had been obliged to make a big enough space for a human body to pass. So far then no difficulty was encountered. But the raiders now came to the foot (*H*) of the vertical drop (just over forty feet) which was very narrow. It was by this conduit that the Jebusites, using a rope, let down the water-skins, held open by circles of wood, and filled them with water. Some historians have refused to believe that Joab and his small band of warriors could have managed to climb up this chimney; they hold that it would have proved an insuperable obstacle. This must also have been the view of the Jebusites. Two English members of the Parker mission answered this sceptical view: in half an hour and with the help of only three wooden cross pieces they managed to climb from *H* to *F*, thus repeating the exploit of David's men.

Next, from *F* to *D* the attackers had only to follow the gentle slope *E*. At *D*, the passageway for the water drawers became narrower and, still at *D*, there was a drop of about eight and a half feet that, in all probability was usually negotiated by a movable ladder. Even if the ladder had been taken away this little difficulty would hardly have delayed Joab and his men for very long. Very soon the party had only to climb the steps (*C*) cut in the rock which led to *B*. Lastly, through the entrance ramp (*A*) – which the archaeologists have not yet succeeded in uncovering – the assailants burst out on to the Ophel.

This explanation, despite its logical and plausible nature, has encountered opposition. In the first place owing to the slender nature of its textual foundation there are great difficulties of translation and interpretation. In addition, the underground excavations are far from complete. Indeed there exists a second Zinnor which enabled the beseiged Jebusites to obtain water supplies at the base of the rock; but this second corridor, whose general plan is known, has only been explored so far very incompletely on account of the difficulties of excavating beneath an inhabited city. It is therefore unlikely that archaeological investigation will be further carried out on this site in the near future. Although scientific prudence requires that we should await the complete findings of these underground excavations, most biblical scholars believe that the explanation of Joab's expedition given above is the most probable one.

Capture of Jerusalem and occupation of the city

The brevity of the biblical account does not enable us to follow in detail the capture of Jerusalem. From Joab's unexpected appearance from the underground passage to the complete capture of the city we know very little. It is very probable that the Hebrews' primary effort was directed against the citadel (Zion). It is difficult to see how the handful of men coming from the Zinnor could have taken it by storm. In any case Jerusalem fell into the hands of Joab very quickly and he was fully avenged for the insults that the Jebusites had hurled at him shortly beforehand from the ramparts.

Possibly, the Jebusites, defended by a small and ill-trained garrison, quickly came to the conclusion that they had lost and surrendered without much resistance, for, somewhat later, when David held the city, there were some old Canaanite inhabitants (such as Ornan, who is mentioned below) who remained in possession of their properties. It was not the custom in ancient times to show so much generosity towards people who had offered resistance to their conquerors.

It appears that Joab was entrusted with the military organization and the administration of the hill of Ophel. Without further delay David settled in Jerusalem and proclaimed it the capital of his twofold kingdom which had so recently been reunited. He was there in a place that was his own, on the borders of the territories of Judah and Benjamin. It was a stronghold that had never belonged to a tribe of the house of Jacob. And this citadel which for two centuries past had constituted a barrier between the tribes of the north and those of the south had now become a link between the two Hebrew groups. David took with him a considerable group of his devoted soldiers and established his residence in the citadel of Zion.[8] The king of the Hebrews, the sovereign of Judah and Israel, now possessed his own capital city.

David transfers the Ark of the Covenant to Jerusalem

A further stroke of genius on David's part was his decision, shortly after he settled in Jerusalem, to transfer

[8] That is, in the citadel itself; its exact location on the Ophel rock is difficult to determine. There has been a good deal of argument among archaeologists and numerous theories, but agreement is far from being realized.

the Ark of the Covenant there.[9] In future therefore the mountain of Zion was to become the political capital of the united kingdom of Judah and Israel, but in addition, and more especially, the religious capital of the People of God. The Ark of acacia wood, covered with gold leaf, made a little more than two centuries previously at the foot of Sinai by order of Moses at the demand of Yahweh, was regarded by the Hebrews as the throne of Yahweh, the one and invisible God. Although by his two-fold anointing David intended to be proclaimed king before the Lord, he insisted on a public affirmation that the real king of the sons of Jacob was Yahweh. The earthly sovereign was only the servant of God and he had to strive in all his acts to apply and fulfil the Law.

We have obviously come to a turning point in the history of the Chosen People. Through Moses, Yahweh led the tribes of nomad shepherds across the desert towards the Promised Land. Through David, he guided the destiny of the new kingdom made up of city-dwellers and farmers. In their journey across the plains the People of God followed the Ark of the Covenant, carried by the Levites. The People of God, now established in the land 'where milk and honey flowed' would fix their eyes on the holy mountain where dwelt Yahweh, their God who protected them.

Where was the Ark?

After its return by the Philistines the Ark had been taken to Israelite territory, at first to the little village of Beth-shemesh and then to Kiriath-jearim where a humble peasant, Abinadab, had been made its guardian.

[9] We do not know the exact date of this transfer. By comparison of the information provided by certain texts we can perhaps fix the arrival of the Ark of the Covenant in Jerusalem in about the year 1000.

David was not the man to let the Ark fall into oblivion, relegated to a private house in a small village under the care of a family which did not even belong to the tribe of Levi. Directly David announced his plan of bringing back the Ark the elders of the various tribes expressed their enthusiastic approval. It can be seen that David desired to complete his political achievement by an imposing religious gesture, yet there were some who were by no means content, like the priests of Gibeah whose Benjaminite sanctuary was situated very near to Jerusalem. Here were preserved the sacred objects dating from the time of Moses: the Tent of Meeting (the mobile sanctuary of the Hebrews at the time of the 'forty years' in the desert), and the altar of bronze. All these evocative religious relics drew many pilgrims to Gibeah, but what was to become of it if nearby Jerusalem was transformed into a holy city, the repository of the Ark of the Covenant? It would mean the ruin of the sanctuary of Gibeah.

Consequently, the priests of the place found excellent reasons for not associating themselves with the transfer of the Ark to Jerusalem. In addition, they belonged to the tribe of Benjamin from which Saul had come, and these people were reluctant to accept David whom they considered a usurper. Thus they formally refused to take part in the ceremony. David did not insist on their attendance.

'False start' of the Ark of the Covenant

The great day had arrived. David decided to take the Ark of Yahweh Sabaoth up to the mountain of Zion. Thousands of the faithful were gathered at Kiriath-jearim to form the escort of the Ark. As was fitting, David as the conqueror of Jerusalem, was there to lead the triumphal procession.

The Ark was taken out from the house of Abinadab, and placed on a new cart drawn by oxen. Here a ritual error must be pointed out: according to the rules it was essential for the Ark to be transported by the Levites using two transversal bars which were never removed, since even the Levites had not the right to touch the sacred object. Though it must be admitted that these details are possibly a later addition.

The imposing procession went forward to sounds of gladness. In front of the cart walked Abinadab with his two sons by his side. All along the processional route hymns and chants arose, lyres and zithers resounded, and the clashing of sistrum and cymbal was to be heard; tambourines and trumpet blasts punctuated the progress of the Ark.

It is possible that this is the context of the 'Gradual Psalm' (Ps. 132), in which Yahweh himself, with his symbolic dwelling, came to take his glorious place in David's city:

Yahweh, remember David
and all the hardships he suffered,
and the oath he swore to Yahweh,

not to enter tent or house
not to climb into bed,
not to allow himself to sleep,
not even to close his eyes,
until he had found a place for Yahweh,
a home for the Mighty One of Jacob!

Yahweh, go up to your resting place,
you and your ark of power.
Your priests are vesting in virtue
and your devout are shouting for joy.

For Yahweh has chosen Zion,
desiring this to be his home,
'Here will I stay for ever,
this is the house I have chosen.'

The procession was drawing near to Jerusalem and came to the threshing floor of Nacon (this place has not been identified). At that moment the cart tilted dangerously on the uneven path and might have overturned. To prevent the Ark falling to the ground Uzzah, one of Abinadab's sons, tried to steady it. But directly he touched the Ark he fell to the ground, struck dead on account of his sacrilegious action. This event is very characteristic of the beliefs of the period and gives us an idea of the still primitive notion of the sacred, whose purpose was to show the power of Yahweh. *For this crime God struck him down on the spot,* reads the Hebrew text; but the text of the whole paragraph is very corrupt.

The whole procession was filled with horror; it came to a halt. David, who believed that this punishment showed the anger of Yahweh, decided that, at least for the time being, they should not enter the city of Jerusalem. He ordered the Ark to be kept provisionally in the house close to the threshing floor of Nacon, in the house of a private individual Obed-edom. Later on a final decision could be made.

Triumphant entry of the Ark of the Covenant into Jerusalem

For the three months that the Ark remained under the roof of Obed-edom the whole family was much blessed. Reassured by the results of this test David thought that the time had come for the Ark to continue its interrupted journey to Mount Zion.

This time care was taken not to place it on a cart;

according to the Mosaic ritual four Levites bore it in the proper manner on their shoulders by means of two transversal wooden bars. For greater safety, the men entrusted with the sacred burden advanced six paces and then stopped. Nothing abnormal happened. In this way they ascertained that Yahweh agreed with the proposed move. In thanksgiving, on the spot, an ox and a fat sheep were sacrificed. Free now from anxiety the procession went joyfully toward the citadel.

David had put off his royal garments and now wore the ritual ephod, a sort of linen loin cloth, the obligatory sacerdotal costume for the sacrifice which he had just offered on the altar; this ephod would also be necessary when he blessed the people in the name of Yahweh. Thus simply clothed, David took his place at the head of the sacred dancers; there, before the Ark, he leapt, whirled round and danced, while the horns of the Levites sounded and musical instruments of all kinds were played.

Thus the Ark went forward, towards the city. On arrival before the walls the procession had to come to a halt: the gates of Jerusalem were closed. It was a moving scene as the people requested that the house of the king of heaven should be allowed to enter the city of the king of Jerusalem. A signal was given and in alternate choirs those present began the chant of a psalm composed for the occasion of which some verses may have survived in Ps. 24: 7–10.

Gates, raise your arches,
rise you ancient doors,
let the king of glory in!

Who is the king of glory?
Yahweh the strong, the valiant,
Yahweh valiant in battle!

The procession went through the city from north to south and then returned to the terrace to the north of the royal residence. There with much pomp and circumstance the Ark was placed in a tent. The priests of Gibeah, of course, had refrained from coming forward with a present of the Tent of Meeting which had sheltered the Ark in its incredible wanderings on the plain of Sinai. It did not matter; a completely new one was made for the occasion. Before it stood an altar on which David made ready to officiate for the second time that day, at holocausts, thanksgivings and communion sacrifices.

Then in the name of Yahweh Sabaoth he gave the blessing to those present. In conclusion to each of the men and women from Israel and Judah there, he gave as a present a roll of bread, a portion of dates and a raisin cake.

Directly after this public ceremony David returned to his palace where he was to bless his own family. One of the first persons whom he encountered was Michal, his first wife, Saul's daughter. Like all the women of the royal harem she had watched the passing of the procession from behind a barred window, and had been unable to prevent herself sniggering at the sight of the king, her husband, wearing only an ephod, dancing half naked before the Ark. She must have been a rather sour-tempered woman, and the remark she made to the hero of the day was somewhat unexpected: '*What a fine reputation the king of Israel has won himself today, displaying*[10] *himself under the eyes of his servant-maids, as any buffoon might display himself.*' Michal, brought up in the court of Gibeah,

[10] This ephod, probably copied from the Egyptian loincloth, consisted merely of a piece of material knotted at the waist. For the sake of decency the Book of Exodus required priests to wear drawers beneath it.

did not seem to have grasped the profound meaning of the translation of the Ark to Zion; she had regarded it as a merely human spectacle, with the king leaping and capering amid a contemptible crowd. With understandable heat David put matters in their true perspective: '*I was dancing for Yahweh,*' he explained, '*not for them. As Yahweh lives, who chose me in preference to your father and his whole House to make me leader of Israel, Yahweh's people, I shall dance before Yahweh and demean myself even more. In your eyes I may be base, but by the maids you speak of I shall be held in honour.*' They were the words of a believer inspired by a generous and vivid faith. David turned away from this wife (who, after all, had previously saved his life): '*And to the day of her death,* concludes the biblical account, *Michal, the daughter of Saul, had no children.*

Thus the Ark had finally taken its place in the imposing setting formed by Jerusalem. Hitherto, the new capital had remained merely a political capital. With the presence of the Ark within its walls it became the religious centre of the Chosen People as well; the rock of the Ophel made its entrance into the religious history of Israel.

David was anxious that this sacred casket containing the stone Tablets of the Law should not return to that partial obscurity which had surrounded it for so long. He wanted the Ark to become a centre of attraction for the faithful of Yahweh, who would come in pilgrimage to pay it devout homage. An imposing form of worship, a moving liturgy, was organized around this important relic. Many Hebrews went up to Jerusalem; when they came down from it and returned to their homes they were dazzled by all they had witnessed and, by the same token, were more firmly attached to the royal house, whose majesty they had been able to admire.

There is no need to exaggerate here; if David's ulterior motives are undeniable, it is true nonetheless that he was animated by a profound faith which was sincere and radiant. He possessed a clear understanding of his responsibilities as leader of the Chosen People in relation to Yahweh. It was through him that Jerusalem became the holy city.

David and the beginning of royal Messianism

Right beside the king's palace within the citadel of Zion, stood the Ark of the Covenant of Moses, the throne of Yahweh, invisible and present. David, who was devout, concerned himself continually about the worship to be paid to Yahweh, the protector of the house of Jacob. One day he had the prophet Nathan summoned to his presence to discuss this question.

Nathan is a new character who now comes on the scene. He was called on to play a role of the highest importance at David's and Solomon's court in the spiritual, religious and even the political spheres. David appears to have adopted him as adviser in certain very difficult cases. On occasion Nathan had no hesitation in admonishing the king severely. For the time being, however, he was merely called in consultation about the project of building the temple.

David spoke: *'Look,'* he said, *'I am living in a house of cedar while the Ark of God dwells in a tent.'* Nathan considered the king's remark to be a very proper one in the circumstances. *'Go and do all that is in your mind,'* he replied, *'for Yahweh is with you.'* Was David to be the founder of the Temple?

Yahweh does not allow David to build the Temple

The next day, of his own accord, Nathan came into the king's presence to inform him of a revelation that he had received during the night. The substance of the message was that it was not to be David who would build a house in stone for Yahweh, it was Yahweh who would build a (genealogical) royal house for David. This was a revelation which in some sort connects the whole plan of the Old Testament with the beginning of the New.

Yahweh 'refused' the building which David proposed to put up to shelter the Ark, the reason being given that for a long time Yahweh had lived *a wanderer's life in a tent*, and never had he told the Judges, *appointed as shepherds of Israel*, to build him a sanctuary of cedar wood. Yahweh showed his disapproval of a permanent building and seemed to want to retain the nomad customs of the wilderness. This reason, as it is given by the biblical writer, seems difficult to accept: in the time of Solomon Yahweh agreed to the idea of a temple to be built in Jerusalem, but the same arguments put forward previously still keep their force. A different explanation, that given in Chronicles, seems preferable; there it is David himself, when he was very old and near to death, who explained the matter to Solomon, his heir: '*My son, my heart was set on building a house for the name of Yahweh my God. But the word of Yahweh came to me* (probably through the prophet Nathan), "*You have shed much blood and fought great battles; it is not for you to build a house for my name, since you have shed so much blood on the earth in my presence*"' (1 Chron. 22: 7–8). Later on David returns to the matter: '*I have made preparations for building, but God has said to me,* "*You are not to build a house for my name, for you have been a man of war and have shed blood*"' (1 Chron. 28: 2–3).

The king went on to explain that by Yahweh's express will it was Solomon, heir to the crown, who would be charged with building the Temple. Later still, on Yahweh's orders (again very probably through the mouth of Nathan the prophet) David was to bequeath to Solomon not only many gold and silver ingots intended to constitute the treasury of the Temple and to ensure the construction of the splendid liturgical furniture, but also the detailed plans of the sanctuary in which the Ark of the Covenant was to rest. Yahweh no longer spoke of his desire that the Ark should remain in a tent. Quite certainly it was the blood that had been shed – and there was a great quantity of it – which was the deciding factor.[11]

The blow to David was a heavy one. As if to soften it the second part of Nathan's message informed David of something quite extraordinary: Yahweh was to grant a remarkable favour to David's descendants: *'Your House and your sovereignty will always stand secure before me and your throne be established for ever.'*

David then went into the tent where the Ark was and, in eastern fashion, seated himself on the ground to pray (2 Sam. 7: 18–29):

'Who am I, Lord Yahweh, and what is my House, that you have led me as far as this? Yet in your sight, Lord Yahweh, this is still not far enough, and you make your promises to extend to the House of your servant for a far distant future. . . . There is none like you, no God but you alone, as our own ears have heard. . . . You have constituted your people Israel to be your own people for ever. . . . Yes, Lord Yahweh, you are God indeed, your words are true and you have given this fair promise to your servant. . . . For you, Lord

[11] Here again we have two divergent traditions which the biblical writer, drawing on different literary sources, has set side by side without trying to combine them.

Yahweh, have spoken and with your blessing the House of your servant will be for ever blessed.'

Messianism

The revelation communicated to David by Nathan must be regarded as one of the theological turning-points of the Old Testament. In addition the Christian can there perceive an important key to the New Testament.

David had just been assured that his dynasty was to be perpetuated on the throne of Jerusalem to the end of time: the whole line of his descendants would remain under Yahweh's protection and he would lead them, uphold them and advise them as his own sons. God's plan had appeared in its clarity; by this uninterrupted succession of princes, called to follow the Law, Yahweh would finally establish his own kingdom on this earth.

This is what biblical scholars term 'Royal Messianism'. Before we examine it we must look at the methods by which David made ready to follow the desires of the Most High.

Psalm 110 ('the priesthood of the Messiah'), in its primitive form at least, explains how David regarded the earthly kingship and the spiritual priesthood imparted to him by God:

Yahweh's oracle to you, my Lord . . .
'I will make your enemies a footstall for you'.[12]

The Lord is at your right hand.
When he grows angry he shatters kings,
he gives the nations their deserts,

[12] Several Egyptian thrones show, on the step placed at the base of the royal seat, forms of foreigners, either painted or drawn, as symbolic representations of vanquished peoples. Thus the sovereign's enemies become his footstool.

smashing their skulls, he heaps the wide world with corpses.[13]
Drinking from the stream as he goes,
he can hold his head high in victory.

We have here, then, a series of invocations which the Christian may use for the theme of his meditation. But the author was speaking at the material level. According to this Psalm, David intended to follow the directions given him by Nathan to the letter: to ensure that the young kingdom was strong Zion had to triumph over its enemies. It meant more wars, more massacres, more battles, more bloodshed. Indeed, at this still very primitive period David could hardly have understood Messianism in any other way.

The Messianic expectation

This, for Israel, meant the great and dynamic hope of the reign of God on earth. It would be established by one of the house of David (called the Messiah, the anointed or consecrated one; at a later date he would be regarded as the Saviour who was to come). All through its turbulent history Israel looked forward to this new age which was to be marked by the restoration of the earthly kingdom of the Hebrews. The defects of successive kings, the historical internal conflicts did not matter. As misfortune after misfortune fell upon the Chosen People, they became all the more attached to the idea of the coming of another David.

Prophets and psalmists, in forms that were constantly developing, gave expression to the same hope; one day Israel would be restored, both spiritually and

[13] A characteristically oriental image, corresponding to horrible scenes represented on the bas-reliefs of the Assyrians, past masters in war. For the historian this provides confirmation of David's bloodthirsty and warlike character. For the Christian reader of the Psalms a spiritual interpretation is necessary: this passage can be understood as divine reprobation of sin.

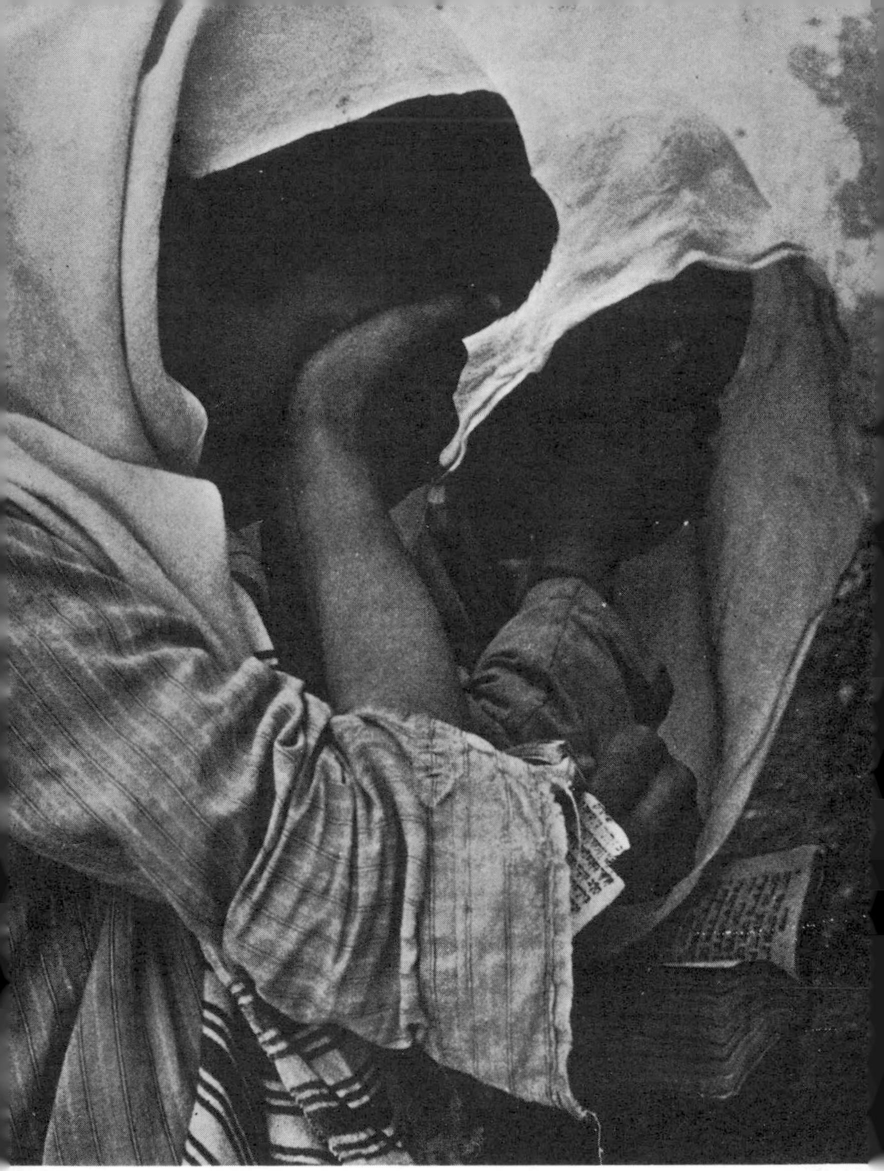

Above the heavens is your majesty chanted
by the mouths of children, babes in arms . . .
I look up at your heavens, made by your fingers,
at the moon and stars you set in place—
ah, what is man . . .
the son of man that you should care for him . . .
Yahweh, our Lord,
how great your name throughout the earth!

Psalm 8

materially, its oppressors would be destroyed and God's justice would reign on earth. Yahweh would be victorious, finally, in Zion.

Theology is not our main concern here. But the historian of religions may perhaps be allowed to state in a few words the fundamental difference that there appears to be between Hebrew and Christian Messianism. Whereas the Israelite regarded David as prefiguring the Messiah, who is still awaited even now, the New Testament asserts clearly that Jesus of Nazareth accomplished Nathan's prophecy to the full. When on Palm Sunday the people of Jerusalem acclaimed Jesus (born at Bethlehem, the city of David) as 'son of David' they acknowledged in this way his title as Messiah. For the Christian, Jesus, 'the son of David' is also 'the Son of God'. He too received a crown (the crown of thorns) at Jerusalem. When Pilate asked whether, as it was rumoured, he was a king, Jesus answered, 'It is you who say it'. He was a king, not of a small nation but of the universal Jerusalem, the symbol of Christianity.

David and his soldiers

David's royal Messianism is shown, it should be emphasized, by his military character. We must always be careful not to judge his century by our own. David's dynamic and constructive genius was essentially of a military character. In addition, his urgent task in the circumstances was to lay the material foundations, as firm and deep as possible, of the nation formed by Israel and Judah. As a result, Solomon, David's son and successor, was able to build on these foundations a wonderful social, political and religious edifice which became the subject of admiration for generations.

David, as we have just seen, succeeded in eliminating

from the field of Hebrew history both the Philistines and the Canaanites. There still remained on the frontiers small kingdoms which continued to cause anxiety to the Hebrews. David's second task was to attack and destroy them. So there were more long and arduous wars before the final victory was won. The kingdom of Israel-Judah then attained dimensions greater than ever before. Before following the Israelite armies on these further expeditions (which will be confined to a description of their principal features only) we can take a closer look at the constitution of these military forces to which David, on a last analysis, owed his success and which worked so effectively for the glory of the greatest king of Israel.

The head of the army

In principle David was commander-in-chief; for some time past he had led his band of adventurers and outlaws into battle and on raids. Nevertheless, since he had become king, and as the complexity of political business absorbed a great part of his activity, he progressively delegated his military functions to Joab, his nephew. Thus the latter soon became the head of the royal army.

In ancient times in the East the highest grades were reserved to members of the royal family. It so happened that Joab was well qualified to assume the responsibilities which now fell to him. Although it is difficult to distinguish between David's personal victories and those of his chief of staff, it is very probable that Joab was personally responsible for a considerable number of successes. The gratitude shown by David in this respect is striking proof of this, all the more since there was little love lost between the two men so that David's praise and congratulations could not be regarded as mere courtesy.

In character, Joab was the exact opposite to David. David was a clever diplomat, a great captain who evoked enthusiasm from his soldiers on account of his attractive personality and the justice and humanity which inspired his actions. Joab, on the other hand, appears to have been a relentless soldier, a man of violence, who imposed his will on all his subordinates without a care for the distress that he caused or the hate which he sowed around him. In battle a fine soldier, he was an unequalled tactician, a cunning leader, and brave (we saw him at work in the Zinnor operation at the capture of Jerusalem), but he remained essentially an uncouth barbarian. Thus when he treacherously slew Abner he took over the commandment of the Israelite troops without asking their opinion; they did not dare make the slightest protest and so they followed the man who had killed their leader. There was no arguing with Joab, he had to be obeyed.

Thus it can be well understood why, despite their very different characters, David entrusted his nephew with command of the army; it could not be in better hands.

David's orders of knighthood

Some time before he was anointed at Hebron David had already established what amounted to an order of knighthood with grades which were granted as a reward for individual exploits. The text of the Bible is not always very explicit on the subject, but there is sufficient evidence to make the position clear.

At the head of this military organization we find the Three whose leader was Abishai. We possess the list of these heroes among heroes and of their mighty deeds (2 Sam. 23: 8–10).

Next, a little inferior in rank came the Thirty. Their

names and places of origin are given after the preceding list (23: 24–39). Their leader at one time was Asahel, Joab's brother; he fell, it will be remembered, to Abner's spear.

From time to time in Chronicles we find mention of the Champions (gibborim) of David. Among these famous warriors, whose exploits were acclaimed in the popular tales told at night in the camps, we find the names of the Three, of course, some of the Thirty and also of men belonging to foreign tribes which had thrown in their lot with David. These Champions probably came from the soldiers who followed and assisted David with such enthusiasm when he was pursued by Saul. In his company, subsequently, they fought against the Philistines and then against the nomads of the desert. They even took the field against Israel before the two kingdoms were united. These Champions do not appear necessarily to have constituted an autonomous body. They may well have served as leaders and officers of the territorial army which is mentioned below.

There is also mention of squires or arms-bearers, whose function was to carry the shield of their leader when they protected him from the enemies' javelins and lances. David began his career by being Saul's arms-bearer. In performing these subordinate functions, which required a certain skill, the young soldiers were trained under a veteran in the secrets of battle by taking an active part in the hand-to-hand fighting. The best and most valiant arms-bearers were chosen to fill the gaps after a heavy battle.

In addition, the Hebrew text uses a word that biblical scholars translate in different ways; some prefer to interpret it as 'personal guard' while others use the term 'military adviser'. Both offices must have existed, we may be sure, but we are not very well informed about their functions.

There was thus a military caste, ready to shed its blood and always ready, also, to receive promotion, titles, and rewards in the shape of agricultural land, vineyards and olive groves.

The two regular armies

As a general rule the Thirty and their arms-bearers were of Hebrew origin. On the other hand, the two bodies of regular troops, the shock troops, were formed of foreign elements; one was formed of non-Semitic elements and the other exclusively of Philistines.

The first was a sort of foreign legion in which David enrolled subjects who by race did not belong to the Middle East: Cretans, Aegeans, Pelethites, representatives of the great heterogeneous family the 'Peoples of the Sea'; the Zekals (or Zakkalas) together with the Philistines. These tough warriors, whose fathers at the beginning of the twelfth century had vainly attempted to seize the Egyptian Delta, had often become excellent farmers; but their real vocation was always for battle and conquest. And so we find a number of their descendants joining David's troops as mercenaries. They were excellent recruits.

The second militia was formed exclusively of Philistines. They were the six hundred men from Gath; after the conquest of their city David enrolled them and brought them back, together with their families to Jerusalem; he had no more faithful supporters than they.

The territorial contingents

With the Champions and the two foreign militias David had at his disposal two thousand men, well-tried soldiers who were almost continually at war.

In addition to these picked men, ready to intervene at the first threat of trouble, the army included territorial contingents, citizens or peasants who were called on from time to time or accepted as volunteers. In this military organization there were the formations of 'ten, fifty, a hundred, a thousand', with officers from the *gibborim*, old soldiers, well-trained in battle and qualified to lead these recruits. The civilians thus enrolled were divided into two categories: there were the youths who were 'chosen', a term that implies preliminary physical examination, and the main body, more or less ready to take part in battle. These two groups were sent into action together or separately according to circumstances.

In company with David's soldiers

Presumably the Thirty and, to a certain extent the Champions and the foreign militia, had at their disposal equipment of high quality – both offensive (sword, lance, javelin) and defensive (helmet, breastplate, leg-guards and a wooden shield covered with leather). The great victories won by these formidable troops had enabled them to obtain rich trophies in the shape of arms taken from their enemies who fell in battle or of the plunder obtained from the Philistine citadels taken by assault.

Far poorer were the arms of those 'called up' on a temporary basis, for a specific campaign. Each of these soldiers was obliged to equip himself at his own expense. Some landed proprietors took pride, of course, in arriving at the meeting place with fine arms. But the small city artisans and the agricultural labourers were often provided with ox goads (well-sharpened, it is true, and feared by their enemies), with rough lances, wooden bows and a quiver with flint-headed arrows (rarely bronze or iron). Some had bludgeons, or axes straight from the farm. Those who were the best equipped proudly wore a short, two-edged sword, hanging from their belt or shoulder belt. The shepherds of the plains, expert in the use of the sling, were sometimes placed together in a special formation. Their function was to make stones rain down on the enemy before hand-to-hand fighting began. On occasion they were sent in pursuit of a fleeing enemy and their missiles rarely missed their aim.

The archers were recruited principally in Benjamin (Judg. 20: 16). In Naphtali the men were usually armed with javelin and lance (1 Chron. 12: 35).

It is curious that the chariot, in common use among the Philistines, which caused terror in the ranks of Hebrew soldiers, was only adopted in Israel at a later period than David, during the time of Solomon.

Pitched battle took place according to a well-defined plan. The two lines of combatants took up their positions so far as possible on facing slopes of a valley. A little behind the line of combatants stood the camp, consisting of tents surrounded by carts containing arms and food; throughout the day a band of soldiers kept careful guard over it. At night sentries, relieved three times during the course of duty, kept watch. At sundown the army retired to the camp for rest; at dawn it returned to its positions. The two opposing forces stood face to face. For some days they shouted insults at each other. Hardened warriors came out in front of the opposing lines to challenge the bravest of the enemy to single combat. Here and there isolated actions took place which eventually degenerated into general battle. On occasion, at a time when the enemy least expected it, the leader decided to launch a general attack; woe to the side which was not ready to receive the wave of assailants, shouting ferociously while the sombre note of the horns resounded over the battlefield. In general, tactics were of a simple nature. Two or three well-tried plans were known and they were put into practice as cunningly as possible.

We have already had a typical example of a war of siege in the investiture of Jerusalem by David. Usually the assailant confined himself to surrounding the city with his forces; after cutting all the city's communications with the outside world he waited patiently for the besieged to be brought to their knees by famine or lack of water (if the city had not been established near a spring). There were no engines of war like those used later by the Romans to reduce fortified towns; there were no catapults nor ballista.

While on campaign a soldier could not count on a regular supply of food. He managed as best he could by looting and pillaging. The state of the countryside after the passage of large forces can be imagined. Generally, armies were confined to a few thousand men.

David knew that he was under the protection of Yahweh; and David's success had convinced all his followers that the God of Armies fought among them and unfailingly brought them victory. The whole strength of Judah-Israel, as David proclaimed on all occasions, was Yahweh, the 'shield' who protected them, the 'Rock' from which they could defy all the assaults of the enemy, the 'inaccessible place' where the wiles of the enemy could not surprise them. Although nowadays the Christian endows with a spiritual meaning such military passages in the Psalms, David and his army understood them in an entirely material way. David's soldiers were convinced that their leader was fighting, on a last analysis, for the establishment of the law of Yahweh, since war was fundamentally religious. The 'holy war' of the Arabs is far from being an Islamic institution; it dates back several thousand years before our era.

David and the wars outside the country

David had succeeded in pacifying the land known as Palestine by the elimination or assimilation of its Canaanite and Philistine populations. But his military role did not end there. To the north, east and south Israel was surrounded by a series of petty kingdoms which did not hide their anxiety in the face of David's increasing power. The new strongly-centralized and well-organized kingdom of Israel-Judah, ruled by an intelligent and ambitious sovereign, caused defensive coalitions between the neighbouring states. As a result there followed for David ten long years of arduous struggle before he achieved final victory.

The following is a summary of the campaigns which David was obliged to conduct outside his own frontiers (see map, over):

Against the Moabites, to the east of the Dead Sea (2 Sam. 8: 1–2);
Against the Syrians (2 Sam. 8: 3–12);
Against the Edomites in the Negeb, between Beersheba and the Dead Sea in the Valley of Salt (2 Sam. 8: 13);
Against the Ammonites in Transjordania (2 Sam. 10: 1–14);
Against the Syrians again (2 Sam. 11: 1; 12:31).

Most of these campaigns were not led into the field by David himself but by the unwearying Joab, David's chief of staff.

The result of these campaigns from the territorial aspect was far beyond what could have been hoped for. In a decade the united kingdom was extended to a degree that was never to be repeated even at the

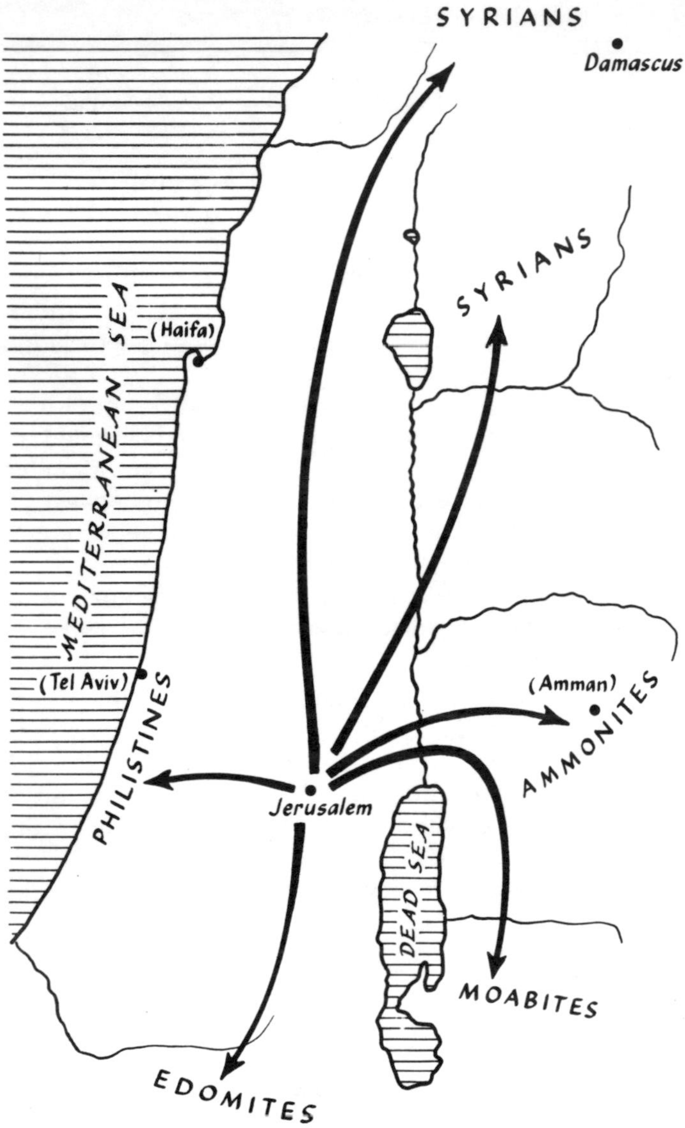

SKETCH MAP OF THE PRINCIPAL CAMPAIGNS OUTSIDE COUNTRY OF DAVID, KING OF ISRAEL AND JUDAH

time of Solomon. Not only was the Promised Land ('from Dan to Beersheba' according to the classic phrase) in the hands of the Israelites, but in addition its frontiers were solidly established to the north, east and south. The peoples who formerly constituted a considerable threat were decimated, humbled, brought into subjection or at least rendered powerless by fear of reprisals; or else they were reduced to accepting an alliance with David.

The enormous booty amassed by the conquerors, and the tribute regularly paid by the vassal countries, increased the wealth of the kingdom of Israel-Judah very quickly. As a result agriculture and trade underwent intensive development. David could be proud of his work.

David's sin

Every hero has his weaknesses and failures. In David's case the failure was conspicuously bad. David, the devout king, who ruled as God's anointed, and upheld the Law of Moses, committed adultery and murder. The opportunity occurred at the time when Joab was waging the second war against the Ammonites, and had laid siege to Rabbah. It was David's misfortune to have remained at Jerusalem.

One summer evening David had just got up from his long siesta – an indispensable rest during the hot season. After the suffocating heat of the day he went to take the air on the palace terrace. The terraces of the houses, standing close together, enabled him to see what was happening on the flat roofs below, and as the palace stood higher than the other buildings the king was in a position to overlook most of his city.

On a terrace not far away he observed a young woman – she was very beautiful the Bible tells us –

It happened towards evening when David had risen from his couch and was strolling on the palace roof, but he saw from the roof a woman bathing; the woman was very beautiful . . . David sent messengers and had her brought.

2 Sam. 2–4

taking a bath. The king inquired about her from his servants. He learnt that her name was Bathsheba; she was, he was told, the wife of Uriah, a Hittite warrior, one of the Thirty, who was with Joab in Transjordania laying siege to Rabbah.

David was impulsive, a man who gave in easily to his own desires. He sent for the woman. As the husband was absent, meetings were frequent until the day came when the unfaithful wife was obliged to confess to her lover that she was pregnant. Uriah had been at the wars for some months and would not normally return to Jerusalem until the completion of the siege.

David endeavours to avoid scandal

David, a cunning diplomat, thought he could avoid the consequences of his adultery. At once he sent a messenger to Joab requesting him to send Uriah the Hittite on the pretext of obtaining news of how the war was going. Uriah gave him good news of the army. David dismissed him, giving him permission to go home to visit his family. Uriah took care not to do so. Among Semite warriors there was a religious law requiring combatants during a war to remain in a state of ritual purity and to abstain from intercourse with women. By not visiting Bathsheba, his wife, as David had treacherously advised him, Uriah was conforming with prescribed custom. In addition, it may well be that he had been informed by well-intentioned friends of his wife's behaviour. In any case, Uriah did not go down to his house; he spent the night at the door of the palace with the guards, his companions in arms whom he knew well. The palace servants reported to David what Uriah had done. David, irritated by the turn of events, sent for Uriah and pretended to be surprised that he had not gone home, as he had been advised. The answer which was given was a veiled one but praiseworthy. Uriah's companions besieging Rabbah were lodged in tents; even the Ark of Yahweh had only a tent in which to dwell, was he to take his ease in a bed? *'As Yahweh lives,'* he protested to the king, *'and as you yourself live, I will do no such thing!'*

David had not yet lost all hope. *'Stay on here today,'* he said, *'tomorrow I will send you back.'* The next day David invited Uriah to his table, gave him a great deal to drink and made him drunk, but Uriah again slept with the palace guard.

The situation had become desperate. Since Uriah refused to take on the fatherhood of the child to be born nothing remained but to make preparations for his disappearance. Joab, in command of the army, was not surprised to receive orders that he was to *station Uriah in the thick of the fight and then fall back behind him so that he may be struck down and die*. Joab soon organized the matter: a skirmish was cunningly arranged and Uriah fell beneath the blows of the besieged enemy. In this way David was delivered from a husband who might have proved awkward.

Bathsheba learned of her husband's death. For seven days she kept faithfully to the prescribed ritual mourning, then David sent for her, she was taken to the palace and entered the king's harem where she became, obviously, his favourite wife. *But what David had done,* says the Bible *displeased Yahweh*.

Nathan's fable and David's verdict

David could hardly hope that his sordid intrigue would remain known only to a small group. Very soon the whole palace was acquainted with the facts. Thereupon the prophet Nathan waited on David; in eastern fashion he recounted this fable to him.

In the same town were two men,
one rich, the other poor.
The rich man had flocks and herds
in great abundance;
the poor man had nothing but a ewe lamb,
one only, a small one he had bought.
This he fed, and it grew up with him and his children,
eating his bread, drinking from his cup,
sleeping on his breast; it was like a daughter to him.
When there came a traveller to stay, the rich man
refused to take one of his own flock or herd
to provide the wayfarer who had come to him.
Instead he took the poor man's lamb
and prepared it for his guest.

From time to time David was called on to give judgement: litigants who thought that they had not received justice from the local chieftains were freely admitted to the palace where they came to appeal to the king. He then examined the matter put before him and set aside or confirmed the previous verdict.

Thinking that Nathan was telling him of a lawsuit David, overcome by anger, rose impatiently from his seat and gave his judgement: *'As Yahweh lives,'* he said, *'the man who did this deserves to die. He must make fourfold restitution for the lamb, for doing such a thing and showing no compassion.'* Nathan said to David, *'You are the man!'*

Yahweh speaks by the mouth of his prophet Nathan

The prophet then changed his tone – he delivered a message in the name of Yahweh; it was the God of Israel speaking to David:

'You are the man.'

The intrepid prophet was transformed into a vehement accuser. He reminded David, the former herdsman of

Bethlehem, how he had been chosen and anointed by Samuel. Yahweh had given him the House of Judah and of Israel. He reminded David of the favours bestowed upon him and the extraordinary destiny awaiting his posterity. To all these great benefits David had replied with treachery and crime. In the name of Yahweh Nathan taxed David with his adultery and the murder of Uriah whom he had betrayed to the sword of the Ammonites.

Prostrate before the man of God, David listened with terror to the account of his crimes.

The message had not yet finished, justice would be done. In the king's own house Yahweh would cause great misfortunes. In David's own lifetime his wives would become the prey of one of his near relations.[14] '*Now the sword will never be far from your own House*.[15]

Remorse, forgiveness – and sanctions

As Nathan went on speaking, the king's conscience was overcome by remorse. There was no argument, no excuses to put forward. The confession came straight from the heart: '*I have sinned against Yahweh*.' Nathan could read the king's conscience very clearly. Divine mercy was about to come into operation; once more Yahweh was to speak through the mouth of his prophet: '*Yahweh forgives your sin . . . yet because you have outraged Yahweh by doing this, the child that is born to you is to die*.' And then, the Bible concludes, Nathan went home.

During the child's illness David was filled with despair. Confessing his sin, he implored Yahweh to spare the

[14] This referred in somewhat mysterious terms to the open revolt which at a later date Absalom started against his father. On this occasion he seized part of David's harem.

[15] A prophecy about the death by the sword of three of David's sons whom he loved especially: Amnon, Absalom and Adonijah. It was a prophecy also about the dark years preceding David's death.

innocent child. He undertook a rigorous fast, and slept on the bare ground. But the relentless punishment followed nonetheless; David was punished through the deepest of his affections; Bathsheba's child was taken from him.

David's sin and Psalm 51

Psalm 51, known as the *Miserere,* bears the following title in the Hebrew text: *Of David. When the prophet Nathan came to him because he had been with Bathsheba*. It forms part of the magnificent series of 'Penitential Psalms'.

Can this Psalm be attributed with certainty to David? Some biblical scholars are inclined to doubt it. They argue that it is surprising to find so profound a religious sense in this Psalm. They consider that this Psalm is much nearer the prophetic literature of the time of Isaiah's (740–700) or Ezekiel's (593–571) ministry. But a careful examination of the texts proves that the lyrical movement of the Psalm – a genuine cry from a soul terror-stricken at the thought of its own sin – is in close correspondence with the historical theme of the tragedy related above. It is this which leads other biblical scholars[16] to the conclusion that Psalm 51 is an authentic Psalm of David; they acknowledge, of course, that the two last verses were added after the return from Babylonian Exile (538 B.C.) and that the whole psalm was possibly revised, at least in some of its poetical expressions, under the influence of the prophets.

David's remorse was sincere and deep, nevertheless, until his death, he was to bear the burden of his twofold crime. According to the theological ideas of the period

[16] Here the conclusions of Fr Tamisier, P.S.S., are followed. And this is done whenever it is a question of the exegesis of the Psalms.

he was to expiate it by fearful trials during the last years of his life.

David's administrative services

Until the capture of Jerusalem David stood out as a soldier, a war leader, always in readiness to go to battle. But after he was established in his new capital he was almost continuously detained in his capital by the administrative needs of the new kingdom of Israel-Judah.

From the military point of view he was well served. Joab, the commander in chief of the national armies, led the expeditions on foreign soil with rare ability. And Benaiah, one of the Thirty, was in command of the foreign troops, the Cherethites and Pelethites. Thus there was no cause for concern in this department.

Forced labour[17] was beginning to be introduced under the direction of Adoram, one of the ministers. The scribe Sheva (possibly an Aramean with a thorough knowledge of Hebrew and cuneiform writing), as secretary, was probably in charge of the accountancy in connection with the possessions of the crown and of the diplomatic correspondence. Jehoshaphat was recorder; he was probably responsible for preparing matters of business, clarifying them and explaining them or summarizing them for the king before or during the meeting of the council. The council consisted of Ahitophel the Judean (who later was to betray David and join Absalom's faction), Hushai, thought by historians not to have been a Hebrew, Jonathan, David's paternal uncle, together with two other inspired persons,

[17] Taxes in money were almost non-existent at this period. A taxpayer gave his help to the State by means of 'days of work' for the king. But in David's time forced labour was still not very arduous; it was to become so in the reign of Solomon.

Nathan, whom we have already encountered and Gad, the 'king's seer'.

On the religious side there were two priests, at the head of the priesthood, Zadok (a new figure, not previously mentioned in the Bible) and Abiathar, who escaped from the massacre of Nob and followed David in his adventurous life after his flight from Saul's court. Zadok and Abiathar are mentioned as 'servants of the kings'; in other words their role was a relatively unimportant one under this theocratic government in which David appeared as the sole representative of Yahweh.

The royal harem and children

One of the most important signs of the power of an oriental sovereign was the number of women – wives or concubines – that he had in his harem. After his enthronement at Hebron as king of Judah, and then as king of Israel, David at once proceeded, as we saw, to set up a harem worthy of a sovereign. During the seven years of his reign in his first capital (1010–1004) he had six sons (2 Sam. 3: 2–5). That was only a beginning. At Jerusalem, as a sign of his prestige and fame, he at once proceeded to take more wives and concubines; thirteen children were born to him. Bathsheba, his favourite wife, lost no time in giving him a second son, who lived, and was to become famous under the name of Solomon. He was David's tenth son, and at this period he could hardly hope to succeed his father on the throne. But in the background there still remained his mother, the astute Bathsheba.

Among David's children who were to be called one day to play an important part in their father's story were four sons and a daughter; Amnon, the eldest; Absalom, the third son, and his sister Tamar, a child of the same mother; Adonijah, the friend of Joab and Abiathar; lastly Solomon, the son of Bathsheba, the friend of Benaiah (commander of the foreign troops), the priest Zadok and the prophet Nathan.

The budget of David's court at Jerusalem

Expenses were heavy: there was the pay of the mercenaries, the salaries of the officials attached to the palace, gifts bestowed here and there in acknowledgement of services rendered, the cost of entertaining, the upkeep of the harem and the various departments of the palace.

As a general rule the people were not called upon to meet these expenses. David was a landed proprietor with considerable revenues. After a victorious campaign against the Philistines or Canaanites he awarded himself large farms, fine vineyards, forests of sycamores, rich olive groves, fields of wheat or barley. When on occasion his subjects rebelled he made confiscations which increased his possessions. In his cellars and barns large quantities of wool and grain were stored and vats of wine and oil. Account must also be taken of the annual tribute exacted from foreign peoples reduced to a state of vassalage.

The former shepherd of the plain of Bethlehem had become the richest proprietor of the kingdom. His court and his state were thus assured of an existence which if not sumptuous was at least worthy of Israel and its king.

David and justice

Usually disputes between individuals were brought before the village chieftains. But the litigant who felt that he had not received justice from a local tribunal could appeal; the king then examined the matter afresh and gave his verdict, which was generally a wise one.

Very rapidly David became known among the people as a just judge, of great humanity, who favoured the weak and needy. Such an attitude was not calculated to please the chieftains and elders in the villages, whose exactions and denials of justice were only too often revealed in this way. Thus in his rebellion against his father, Absalom found a ready ear and eager assistance among the country magistrates who were indignant at finding their sentences overruled by the king.

David and forced labour

A certain caution is necessary, it would appear, on the subject of levies and forced labour at the time of David. It is possible that some requisitions of labourers were made to restore or widen a small part of the walls of Jerusalem, but there was nothing comparable to what took place at this same period, to a degree that was absolutely inhuman, in Mesopotamia and Egypt. Israel had to wait until the following reign, that of Solomon, to obtain an idea of this harsh institution in which men were treated like animals.

The curious affair of the census

In the East to take a census was regarded as a wicked action: God alone had the right to know the exact number of his creatures. In addition, the nomads, like the recently settled residents (and this was the case with the Israelites) were strongly opposed to these controls by the royal power. In their view – and they were usually right – the census paved the way for other kinds of inquiry regarding property, income and so on.

A military census was regarded as sacrilege, and it was precisely such a census that David carried out in order to discover how many men 'able to draw the sword' he could count on. In the first place, the Israelites objected, the country did not belong to David, it was the personal property of Yahweh. His action was therefore anti-religious. In addition, it was contrary to well-established custom: a 'holy war' was waged only on the strength of voluntary service. Why therefore was David taking a census of *all* the men of Judah and Israel? It could only be for the purpose of a general mobilization.

And so, Yahweh punished the king by sending three days' pestilence which ravaged the people; thus the results of the census were vitiated by the fact that after it had taken place thousands of men had been carried off by the pestilence.

While the pestilence was spreading through the kingdom David saw the 'avenging angel' stretching out his hand over Jerusalem to destroy the capital in its turn. Thereupon David addressed a fervent prayer to the Lord, declaring that he alone was guilty. *'It was I who sinned,'* he said, *'I who did this wicked thing. But these, this flock, what have they done? Let your hand lie heavy on me then, and on my family.'* That very day, as if in answer to his prayer, David received a visit from the prophet Gad who gave him this message: he was to go up to the threshing floor of Ornan the Jebusite where the angel of God had been seen to appear; on this spot David was to put up an altar to Yahweh in expiation. The threshing floor of Ornan was a site close to Jerusalem outside the walls, dominating the city to the north.

At once David and his officers took the path leading to this place. Just at this time Ornan, the owner, was threshing his wheat harvest *on a sledge* as the Bible puts it. This was a kind of plank fitted with sharp stones underneath. The man stood on it, and drove the oxen over the circular floor; by this means the grain was separated from the straw and husk, and could be winnowed when the wind blew.

Directly Ornan saw the king approaching he fell

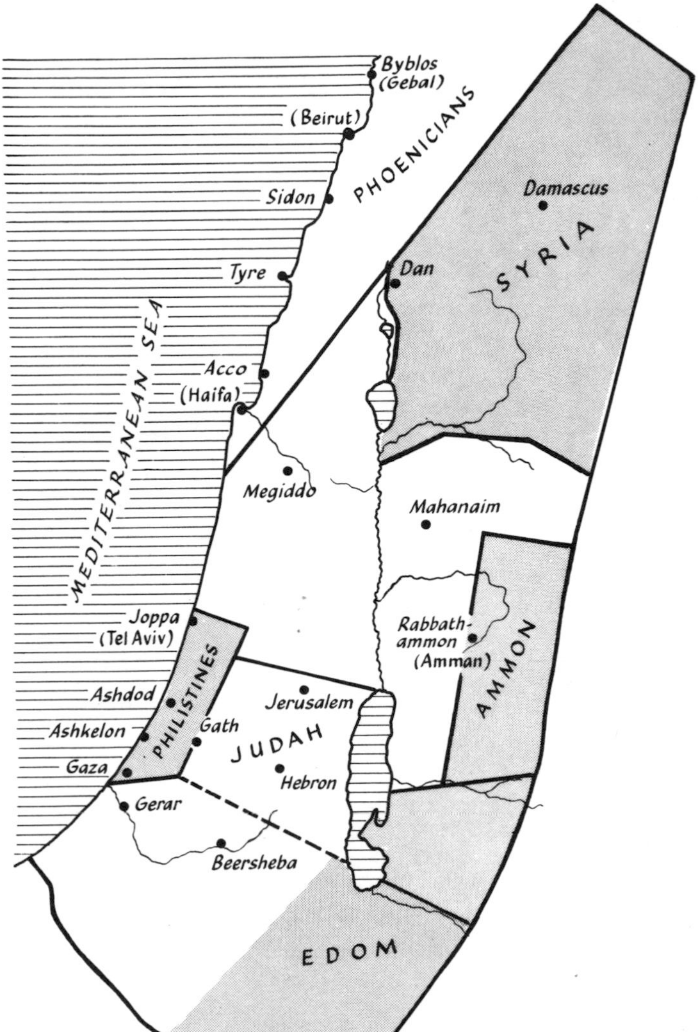

DAVID'S EMPIRE

David's external conquests are marked grey. These annexed territories should more properly be regarded as vassal provinces paying tribute to Jerusalem.

prostrate on the ground before him. When he heard that the king wished to acquire the field to build an altar and preserve the city from the plague, Ornan hastened to offer it to him as a present; that indeed was the custom. Let the king take the land for nothing, together with the oxen for the burnt offering. The wooden sledge could be the fuel. Of course the king could not accept such generosity. *'No, I must pay money for it,'* he said. *'I will not offer Yahweh my God holocausts which have cost me nothing.'* For the threshing floor and the oxen Ornan received fifty shekels.

For the time being quite a simple altar was put up on Ornan's threshing floor. Its history and exact location have been carefully noted here (see map, p. 128) because on this spot Solomon was soon to build the imposing temple of Jerusalem.

6

THE OLD KING (975–970)

David was nearly seventy. He was an old soldier worn out by the strenuous campaigns of his youth and maturity. But he was to be unable to look forward to ending his days in his imposing capital city of Jerusalem in a calm and peaceful atmosphere. His last years were to be clouded by terrible family tragedies and palace revolutions. David had committed two crimes and the simple theology of the period still believed in the exclusively temporal idea of reward or punishment of the creature on this earth. As a consequence, before his death he would have to expiate the evil that he had done.

Violent end of the family of Saul

For three years there had been terrible famine in the kingdom. Interrogation of the oracle (it was probably the ephod, the instrument of divination about which both historian and archaeologist know very little) had revealed that *There is blood on Saul and his family because he put the Gibeonites to death*. This was an old story whose origins went back some two centuries. In the time of Joshua and the invasion of the land of Canaan by the Hebrews the inhabitants of Gibeon (Canaanites) had made a treaty with the Israelites; Joshua had promised the Gibeonites under oath that the Chosen People would always protect them. This was a sacred undertaking, made in the presence of Yahweh. Subsequently Saul, engaged in the task of overcoming the 'foreign' enclaves in the Promised Land had violated the pact and the Gibeonite population had been massacred without mercy.

David hastened to offer to the Gibeonites – the descendants of the survivors of Saul's massacre – monetary compensation. They refused categorically: blood, they answered, demanded blood. They requested, in accordance with the harsh law of the period, that the seven descendants of Saul should be handed over to them. At once they were put to death, dismembered, and their remains exposed on a gibbet in the shape of a fork where the birds could devour them.

Thus the blood of the Gibeonites received satisfaction and from that time the famine ceased. It should not be forgotten that the Gibeonites belonged to the Canaanite religion and, according to an ancient polytheistic belief, human blood restores fertility.

Although this savage execution benefitted the royal house of David, which thus witnessed the disappearance of the last representatives of Saul's family, David was greatly upset by this bloodthirsty ceremony of expiation. It was wholly unjust of his opponents to blame him on several occasions for having contrived it. But this was merely the raising of the curtain. Far more painful trials, of a more personal nature, now awaited the old king.

Absalom, David's second son, openly rebels against his father

Like most of David's family, Absalom was extremely handsome. *From the sole of his foot to the crown of his head there was not a blemish on him*, the Bible tells us. His face was surmounted by a fine head of hair, famous throughout the kingdom. Tamar, Absalom's half-sister, was also of bewitching beauty. Now Amnon, David's eldest son (but not by the same mother as Absalom and Tamar) fell deeply in love with his half-sister; he pretended to be ill and had Tamar sent to him. Despite her cries he overpowered her and raped her, and then had her thrust out into the street.

Frantic with disgust and shame Tamar tore the sleeves of her tunic and covered her head with dust; then, placing her hand on her head (the gesture of mourners) she sought refuge with her brother Absalom. It was not difficult to foresee the end of the tragedy. Indeed, the responsibility for subsequent events was very largely David's, for he seems to have ignored his eldest son's dishonourable behaviour. Towards his sons he was to display very great weakness.

Absalom's vindictive spirit was well known throughout the country, but surprisingly there was no reaction from him at all. Two years after these events, when the sheep-shearers were at Baalhazor, a village near Jerusalem, he cordially invited his brothers to the festivities which traditionally marked the end of this important pastoral operation. Amnon might well have supposed that his younger brother had forgotten what had happened, and so he attended the feast. At the end of the meal, when he least expected it, he was brutally struck down by Absalom's servants. Tamar was avenged.

At once, all the other brothers, believing that they too were in imminent danger, rushed to the stables, jumped on their mules and hurried back to Jerusalem. David thus heard of the tragedy; he wept bitterly for his eldest son. But still showing great weakness he never even protested at Absalom's cowardly action. Absalom, however, had taken flight. Three years later, through the active support of Joab he was allowed to return to

Jerusalem, but his father still refused to receive him at court. Two more years passed. Finally Joab was successful in obtaining Absalom's complete pardon. David gave him the kiss of peace.

There were two consequences of the murder of Amnon: Absalom avenged the injury done to his sister Tamar, but also, by the death of his eldest brother, Absalom became the heir to the crown.

Absalom awaited the death of his father so that he could become king. It seemed to him that the old king was taking a long time to die. Then, too, he had to foil any royal decisions that might be promulgated at the last moment. David, in a very weak physical condition, was quite capable of designating on his deathbed another of his sons as his successor, for at that period the law of primogeniture was by no means firmly established. Absalom had made up his mind; he prepared the ground by gathering round him all those in the kingdom who were discontented. And they were numerous. There were Judaeans who found David far too generous and considerate to the Israelites; there were Israelites who could not get accustomed to the idea of being governed by a Judaean; there were Benjaminites who regarded David as a usurper, and the murderer (it was quite untrue) of the last of Saul's family. Despite all that he had accomplished in the religious, political and military spheres, achievements bearing the stamp of genius, David received only hate and ingratitude. Absalom, using the methods of a cunning demagogue, offered himself to the country with a policy entirely opposed to that of his father. Everywhere he was received with enthusiasm. David was well aware of his son's plotting, but he did nothing, showing in the matter great weakness again.

The die was cast; rebellion broke out. Absalom

assembled his forces at Hebron and marched on Jerusalem. At once almost all the kingdom came out against David in favour of his rebel son. To avoid a fearful encounter David decided to leave Jerusalem and go into exile. Fortunately his army – the Thirty, the *gibborim* and the foreign troops – remained faithful to him. With his soldiers he left the Holy City.

It was a mournful procession. David had not wanted the Ark of the Covenant to leave the city. *'Should I win the favour of Yahweh,'* he said, *'he will bring me back and permit me to see it and its dwelling place again. But should he say, "I take no pleasure in you," then here I am, let him deal with me as he likes.'* His robes torn, his head covered and his feet bare, his face bathed in tears, the old king went down to the valley of Kidron and then up to the Mount of Olives; following the whole procession of people, who were weeping as they went, he set out for Jericho.

In the city he had left ten of his concubines. The priests Zadok and Abiathar, and David's counsellor Hushai had all wished to follow him into exile. Cunningly, David had decided otherwise: his three devoted servants were to remain in Jerusalem where they would pretend to espouse the cause of Absalom. There in the usurper's court they would act as secret agents for the dethroned king, they would give perfidious advice to Absalom and by means of a clandestine organization of messengers would keep David in touch with the political situation.

As the caravan came near to the village of Bahurim a Benjaminite, Shimei, suddenly appeared by the side of the road. He belonged to the same clan as Saul, the late king. When he saw David he began to curse him and insult him. *'Be off, be off, man of blood, scoundrel!'* he exclaimed. And he followed David, throwing stones. Abishai, the leader of the warriors, suggested that he should cut off Shimei's head. The king stopped him. *'Let him curse,'* he said. *'If Yahweh said to him, "Curse David", what right has anyone to say, "Why have you done this?".'* The caravan went sadly on its way.

Absalom was welcomed in Jerusalem with shouts of *Long live the king! Long live the king!'* By his side marched Ahithophel, one of David's friends and counsellors who had betrayed the confidence of his former master. Very soon Absalom was anointed king. Without more ado he seized the harem that his father had left at Jerusalem. This was a political gesture: the conqueror of a king hastened to take possession of the royal harem, for in this way he affirmed and proclaimed his annexation of power. Thus was fulfilled one of the prophecies of Nathan when he foretold this public affront as a punishment for David's adultery with Bathesheba.

At the head of his troops Absalom set off in pursuit of his father. The battle took place near Mahanaim. Before it began David, broken-hearted, besought Joab and the officers of the royal army to spare Absalom, his heir and beloved son, if he came within range of their lances or javelins. Joab shrugged his shoulders. He had a battle to win and he had made up his mind to win it.

Under the leadership of the intrepid Joab the army lost no time in cutting Absalom's army in pieces. Put to rout completely, the rebel forces fled in all directions. Absalom on his mule galloped into the forest. At one place the mule passed under the thick branches of a great oak; its rider's neck was caught inextricably among the branches while the mule went on. Absalom remained hanging, unable to free himself. (He was not caught by his hair, as has frequently, but mistakenly, been reported.) One of David's warriors discovered him in this helpless position; Joab was at once informed and came to the place. Despite the king's urgent request to Joab not to kill Absalom if the chance of battle were to bring the two men face to face, Joab seized three javelins and plunged them into Absalom's heart. Joab's armour-bearers then cut him down, the body was thrown into a deep pit dug in the forest and a great cairn was built over the grave. Then Joab had the signal given on the trumpet announcing the end of the battle.

David heard with relief the news of the victory, but he was stricken with grief when told of his son's death. He began to shudder and weep. He went up to the room over the gate of Mahanaim, covered his head as a sign of mourning and in a terrible fit of despair, forgetting all the wrongs perpetrated by his dead son, cried out aloud. *'My son, Absalom! Absalom, my son, my son!'* This angered Joab. He went up to the room in which the king had taken refuge and spoke sharply: *'You are covering yourself with shame,'* he said. And he led him out to the gate of the city before which the victorious army was parading in triumph.

Then came the return to Jerusalem. Those in the capital who had unwisely acclaimed Absalom now crowded round David, congratulating him on his victory and assuring him of their unshakable loyalty. Unashamedly they vied with each other to pay him all sorts of fullsome compliments. David preferred to show mercy. There was no settling of past accounts, no purge. The king regained his throne – bruised and sorrow-stricken, his soul filled with bitterness.

There was another rebellion. Fortunately, on this occasion the instigator did not belong to the royal family; he was a Benjaminite ('a scoundrel' according to the Bible) of the name of Sheba. Joab, of course, was given the task of quelling this further rebellion. He went in pursuit of the rebel and came up with him in the region of Dan, at the northern border of the land of Israel, laid siege to the citadel in which Sheba had taken refuge and obtained his head. So the matter was settled.

The struggle for the succession

Towards the end of his life, David, who suffered from the cold, hardly left his bed. Though they laid many coverlets on him it seemed impossible to keep out the cold. In an effort to warm him his servants brought to his bed a young concubine, Abishag, the beautiful Shunamite. The remedy was unsuccessful. The king was advancing rapidly towards the grave.

All were wondering who would wear the crown on David's death. Properly speaking, it should have been Adonijah, the third son, since the two elder sons, Amnon and Absalom had died in the tragic circumstances that have been related. Around the heir presumptive a political group was formed ready to further his candidature to the throne by all available means. There was Joab, the constantly victorious commander-in-chief, and the priest Abiathar, a survivor of the massacre at Nob, and David's faithful follower. In addition, there were most of Adonijah's brothers.

Opposed to this party was that of Solomon, the son of Bathsheba, the powerful, insinuating favourite of the king to whom he always listened. On this side too, was the high priest Zadok, the prophet Nathan and Benaiah, the leader of the foreign troops.

It was difficult to see which of these two factions would succeed. With one word David could have settled the question. But as on every occasion when he had to judge between his sons, he hesitated, temporized and kept silent. He again showed the parental weakness which caused him to recoil from causing pain to one of his children. Strong in his right as the eldest son, Adonijah decided to act. Without waiting for his father's death he evolved a cunning plan which would secure, or so he hoped, his proclamation as king and his solemn anointing for this office. He gathered together a numerous body of his partisans by inviting them to a great banquet. This imposing meeting – whose political implications had certainly been grasped by all present – took place by the Fuller's Spring at the Sliding Stone at the south-east corner of the rock of Ophel. At the end of the banquet, when those present were cheered by the wine, Adonijah's friends would shout out, 'Long live the king!' The acclamation would be enthusiastically repeated by the whole company and the trick would have succeeded.

But the opposing party – Bathsheba, Zadok, Nathan and Benaiah – were not to be outdone.

Nathan and Bathsheba's counterstroke

Nathan was rapidly informed of Adonijah's plan. He hastened to Bathsheba. Without a moment's delay their plan was formed.

Bathsheba went to David in his room. Kneeling down she did homage and then reminded David that he had formally promised to place their son Solomon on the throne as his successor. *'And now,'* she observed with well-feigned bitterness, *'here is Adonijah king and you, my lord king, knowing nothing about it.'* She had no illusions on the subject: directly David was sleeping with his fathers, she and their son Solomon would be promptly executed.

Hardly had Bathsheba finished her remarks than Nathan the prophet was announced. He too knelt down and did homage. As we have seen, Nathan could speak forcefully. He made no secret of his painful surprise. He pretended to believe that David had chosen Adonijah as his successor and given orders for his coronation. At that very moment, he said, the royal banquet was in full swing; the royal officers and the priest Abiathar were gleefully shouting, 'Long live the king!' Nathan the prophet, the priest Zadok and Benaiah had been ignored; they had not even been invited to the royal banquet. It seemed that David had treated his old friends, his firmest supporters, in a very off-handed fashion.

The result was not unexpected. David was very angry. Solomon was to reign. Let Zadok the priest and Benaiah, the commander of the guard, be summoned at once. The excitement had restored to the king some of the energy of his youth; he gave precise and urgent orders: *'Take the royal guard with you, mount my son Solomon on my own mule and escort him down to Gihon* (the spring of Gihon at the foot of the citadel). *There Zadok the priest and the prophet Nathan are to anoint him king of Israel; then sound the trumpet and shout, "Long live King Solomon!" Then you are to follow him up and he is to come and take his seat on my throne and be king in place of me, for he is the man I have appointed as ruler of Israel and of Judah.'* and Benaiah answered, *'Amen'*.

The ceremony was performed in accordance with David's orders. In the valley of Kidron, Zadok anointed the new sovereign's forehead with oil. The people, who appeared always to be amenable, acclaimed him with joy: *'Long live King Solomon!'* The trumpets sounded in the narrow valley and the flutes joined in.

Defeat of Adonijah's party

Among Adonijah's guests at the banquet panic reigned. Adonijah, realizing that his life hung on a thread, ran off to the Ophel and entered the tent where the Ark of the Covenant was. There stood there a small altar whose four corners were shaped like horns. Adonijah seized one of these horns and clung to it – this was the gesture of a suppliant who, in the sanctuary of Yahweh, asked for

As David's life drew to a close he laid this charge on his son Solomon, 'I am going the way of all the earth. Be strong and show yourself a man' . . .
So David slept with his ancestors and was buried in the Citadel of David.

1 Kings 2:1–2, 10

sanctuary. In a tone full of contempt Solomon said to him, *'Go to your house'*. Further action could be decided upon later. Joab and the other plotters all went home. It was the best thing they could do.

The Death of David: 970 B.C.

David bowed down on his bed, saying, *'Blessed be Yahweh, the God of Israel, who has allowed my eyes to see one of my descendants sitting on my throne today!'* In fact, it was his own fault that it had not happened sooner; had it been done so many complications would have been avoided.

Shortly afterwards David *slept with his ancestors and was buried in the Citadel of David*. He was seventy years old. His tomb was hollowed out of the rock of Ophel, it appears. It probably forms part of the eastern necropolis of the hill in which several royal tombs have already been discovered.

CONCLUSION

David's chief place in the history of the Near East is that of liberator of the Promised Land. For a thousand years after his reign, the people of the kingdom he had founded worked out their destiny, until a new 'anointed one' was born in Bethlehem.

To accomplish what he had to do, David had shown enormous political abilities, the insight which can sieze the opportunity of the moment and use it for the nation's good. Above all, he had taken advantage of the temporary eclipse of his two mighty neighbours, Egypt to the south and Mesopotamia to the north-east, both of whom were immobilized for the time being by internal troubles. It was a providential respite in the continual power pressures to which Palestine has always been exposed. It enabled David to endow the kingdom of Israel-Judah with national unity, a capital city, and a king who would leave a stable dynasty when he died.

As a politician of very great shrewdness, a military leader of the first order, a realistic organiser and a subtle diplomat, David was a great man by any standards. He was one of those complete, all-round men of outstanding ability, whose like does not occur very often in history.

David gave Hebrew historians their model for the ideal sovereign, the king by which they judged all the kings who came after him. Moses had revealed the Law of Yahweh to the tribes of Israel. David had created a kingdom where men could live by that law and serve Yahweh with single-minded devotion. He was unable to build the Temple of Jerusalem himself, but tradition claimed that he was its originator, that he bequeathed the plans for it to his son Solomon, and established the organization of men who served the Temple. These people, the priests, Levites, singers, and many others, were the living stones of the sacred building which housed the Ark of the Covenant. Later generations of priests may have attributed more to David himself than was achieved during his actual reign, but there can be no doubt that he laid the foundations of the nation as a kingdom which drew its strength from the worship of Yahweh, and that he inspired those who followed him to continue what he had begun.

Both Jews and Christians honour David as the principal author of the Psalms. There is no doubt that his reign stimulated a great period of Hebrew poetry, and that David himself was the leading poet. The tradition which places him at the centre of this great field of ability is very strong indeed, and such examples of his poetry as the lament for Saul and Jonathan, and the lament for Absalom, can still move us deeply. The Psalms were the nation's hymns and prayers, and they have remained one of the most fruitful sources of man's religious life. Many of the Psalms cannot be given an accurate date, and some show the influence of later events than those of David's reign. But all of them reflect the deep personal religion, and the ideals of Yahweh, which David clearly inspired.

The nation had far to go in the understanding of the God who had chosen and protected it, but David created the opportunity which made that understanding possible. The great prophets, who guided later generations towards full and universal monotheism, could look back to David's reign and tell their people that the Messiah, when he came, would bring to its perfection the work which David had begun.

SELECT BIBLIOGRAPHY

The Jerusalem Bible; Darton, Longman & Todd (London), Doubleday and Company (New York)

General Books

A Catholic Commentary on Holy Scripture; Nelson (London)

Peake's Commentary on the Bible (Revised Edition); Nelson (London)

Atlas of the Bible; L. H. Grollenberg, O.P., Nelson (London)

J. Bright, S.J.: *A History of Israel*; S.C.M. Press (London), Westminster Press (Philadelphia)

C. Charlier: *The Christian Approach to the Bible*; Sands Publishers (Glasgow)

L. Johnston: *A History of Israel*; Sheed and Ward (London and New York)

T. Maertens, O.S.B.: *Bible Themes*; Darton, Longman & Todd (London), Fides Publishers (Notre Dame)

J. L. McKenzie, S.J.: *Dictionary of the Bible*; Chapman (London), The Bruce Publishing Company (Milwaukee)

R. de Vaux, O.P.: *Ancient Israel*; Darton, Longman & Todd (London), McGraw Hill (New York)

Select Bibliography

Books about David

H. W. Hertzberg: *I and II Samuel*; S.C.M. Press (London)

J. Rhymer: *The Covenant and the Kingdom*; Sheed and Ward (London)

E. C. Rust: *Judges, Ruth, Samuel*; S.C.M. Press (London), Knox Press (Richmond)

INDEX OF NAMES

INDEX OF PLACES